ZECHARIAH

THE LORD HAS REMEMBERED

MARC WHEWAY PH.D

Ark House Press
arkhousepress.com

© 2022 Marc Wheway Ph.D.

All rights reserved. Apart from any fair dealing for the purpose of study, research, criticism, or review, as permitted under the Copyright Act, no part may be reproduced by any process without written permission.

Unless otherwise stated, all Scriptures are taken from the New International Translation (Holy Bible. Copyright© 1996, 2004, 2007, 2013 by Tyndale House Foundation. Used by permission of Tyndale House Publishers Inc., Carol Stream, Illinois 60188. All rights reserved.)

Some names and identifying details have been changed to protect the privacy of individuals.

Cataloguing in Publication Data:
Title: Zechariah
ISBN: 978-0-6455535-9-8 (pbk)
Subjects: Biblical Studies; End Times; Christian Living;
Other Authors/Contributors: Wheway, Marc Ph.D.

Design by initiateagency.com

CONTENTS

The Coming Kingdom i

Introduction ix

CHAPTER ONE—PART ONE 1
   Repent, Return, Renew 1
   Return and Rebuild 9
   Seek First the Kingdom 17

CHAPTER ONE—PART TWO 20
   The Horseman 20

CHAPTER ONE—PART THREE 25
   Four Horns / Four Craftsmen 25

CHAPTER TWO 33
   The Measuring Line 33

CHAPTER THREE 40
   Joshua the High Priest 40

CHAPTER FOUR 47
   The Two Lampstands 47

CHAPTER FIVE 56
    Flying Scroll 56

CHAPTER SIX—PART ONE 64
    The Four Chariots 64

CHAPTER SIX—PART TWO 71
    The Branch and the Temple 71
    Rebuild the Temple 78

CHAPTER SEVEN 85
    False Worship 85

CHAPER EIGHT 93
    Lasting Peace and Prosperity 93

CHAPTER NINE 100
    Behold, Your King is Coming to You 100

CHAPTER TEN 107
    With a Whistle 107

CHAPTER ELEVEN 115
    Doomed to Slaughter 115

CHAPTER TWELVE—PART ONE 122
    A Cup of Staggering 122

CHAPTER TWELVE—PART TWO 128
    On that Day 128

CHAPTER THIRTEEN 136
    The Shepherd Struck 136

CHAPTER FOURTEEN 146
   The Day of the Lord... 146
   The Riddle of Time.. 156

About the Author.. 168

INTRODUCTION

The theme of the book of Zechariah, like the book of Revelation, is repentance and renewal, preparing for the temple rebuild and the appearing of God's Son. Zechariah's ministry follows Daniel; in chapter nine of his book, Daniel prayed the prayer of repentance for himself and God's people thinking this would be the time of the Messiah. The Jewish people expected the Messiah to come, judge the nations and establish His reign from the holy hill, Jerusalem. Therefore, they must prepare, and be ready. Zechariah ends with the same hope and expectation, "The Lord will be King over all the earth. On that day the Lord will be One and His name One" (Zech. 14:9).

Before the Lord establishes His rule on the earth, a series of events must first take place. Zechariah sees the events through eight night visions, from chapters one to six. Chapter seven focuses on showing kindness and mercy, making ready for God's Son. The following chapters concentrate on the associated events with the coming King.

Zechariah's ministry was purposed to addressed Judah, warning them not to do as their fathers did or else they would suffer the same fate. The problem addressed was idolatry. The solution was to return to God, that He would return to them.

The book Zechariah is the fifth of its kind that the author has written, following The Revelation the Revival, The Revelation, Proclaimed and

Explained, Daniel's Divulgement, and Twenty-Four. The listed published books are the author's continual work on the subject of eschatology after earning a Ph.D. from Louisiana Baptist University.

Like the author's previous books, Zechariah serves the reader, preparing them for the things to come, namely the return of Jesus Christ. Whether the reader is on this side of the tribulation or in it, this book will be an invaluable reference.

CHAPTER ONE—PART ONE

REPENT, RETURN, RENEW

'The Prophets, do they Live Forever'
(Zech. 1:1-6)

Following Judah's release from Babylon, after seventy years of captivity (Dan. 9:2, cf. Jer. 25:12), the people of God return to Jerusalem. There they are instructed to repent, return, and renew their covenant with God (Zech. 1:3) and then get back to rebuilding the temple (Zech. 4:8-10, Hag. 1:8, cf. Ezra 4:24-5:1). The first temple was destroyed by king Nebuchadnezzar seventy years earlier (1 Kgs. 25:8-17). Due to Judah's disobedience, God sent Judah into exile; after forty years of warning them, He would, through the prophet Jeremiah (Jer. 1:2-3). Despite the many warnings, Judah refused to listen for four decades, believing that because they were in covenant with God, He would not judge them, regardless of their actions. Sound familiar? The same line of thinking has plagued the church from its commencement until this day through hyper-grace teaching (i.e., I can do whatever I like, and it will be alright) and through the Calvinistic doctrine, 'Once saved, always saved.'

In the same way, Jeremiah warned Judah, Zechariah now warns the next generation, that if they do what their forefathers did, they will suffer the same fate and they did. Zechariah's message points to the coming Messiah (Zech. 12-14); therefore the call to repentance is in preparation for the coming King. The very idea of the Messiah coming to judge and rule over the Jews and the Gentiles caused Daniel to repent of his sins and the nation's sin (Dan. 9). The same should be true for the church. Remembering, what God did to Israel, He will also do to confessing followers of Christ if they behave in the same way (Rom. 11:22). Further evidence is seen in the book of Hebrews (Heb. 3:7-4:13) and again through the letters written to the seven churches in the book of Revelation (Rev. 2-3). The lesson is that covenantal security requires observance and overcoming obedience (obedience that overcomes).

In sum, five hundred years before Christ, God appointed the prophet Zechariah to call His people to repentance in preparation for His appearance and return. No Old Testament prophet understood that there would be two parts to Christ's coming. Again, the call to repentance follows seventy years of captivity, with blessing and prosperity now in mind. God's prosperity would come through the rebuilt temple, where, once again, His Spirit would dwell with His people. If Judah returned to God, He would then return to them, implying He was not with them now. Judah, now void of God, was given a new start, another opportunity to get right with Him and enjoy the covenant's blessings and benefits, namely, God. The previous generation broke their covenant and was, therefore, cut off from God (Lam. 5:22). Consequently, they were expelled from the Promised Land and lost their inheritance. God often warned the Jews of the coming judgement, but they would not listen (Zech. 1:4, cf. Jer. 35:15), and they did they heed the warnings (Jer. 6:17, 19; 18:18; 23:18).

Note the words, "The word of the Lord came to the prophet" (Zech. 1:1). The phrase "The word of the Lord came" is seen well over one hundred times within scripture and always within the Old Testament. The phrase and statement are seen ten times within the book of Zechariah alone (Zech. 1:1, 7, 4:8, 6:9, 7:1, 4, 8, 12, 8:1, 18). When giving a word from the Lord, the prophet was not 'looking' for one, and neither was he attempting to conjure one up, operating out of his soul or through a demonic spirit.

Zechariah was not like the false prophets of Jeremiah's day (Jer. 27:9) or like the first-century charlatans (Jude 8). He was a true prophet of God. Through the true prophet of God, the word of the Lord comes (cf. Jonah 3:1, Hos. 1:1, Joel 1:1); it burns within and bubbles up - it cannot be contained (Jer. 5:14, 20:9, 23:29). It does not boil over through a forced invoking. Genuine prophecy bubbles up while false prophecy is boiled up. The word 'Prophecy' literally means bubble up. Notice also, that Old Testament prophets never brought a fluffy word (Jer. 5:14), unlike the false, then, and today, who come preaching peace and prosperity.

Genuine prophecy is the very words of God, often introduced with the idiom, "Thus says the Lord." The words, "Thus says the Lord" are found thirty times in the book of Jeremiah, and fifty times, in Jeremiah's colleagues' book, Ezekiel, who wrote from Babylon as one of the exiles. Jeremiah wrote from Jerusalem, for he was not taken captive by king Nebuchadnezzar. From Jerusalem, Jeremiah continued to write to Judah in Babylon, as did Ezekiel from within Babylon. Again, both introduced God's word with, "Thus says the Lord." The prophet Zechariah uses the same idiom as Jeremiah and Ezekiel (Zech. 1:1, 3).

Zechariah was a recognised prophet of God alongside Haggai (Ezra 5:1, 6:14). The prophet Haggai was best known for the phrase, "Consider your ways," only found in the book of Haggai (Hag. 1:5 & 7), with a focus on the temple being rebuild (Hag. 1:7). Like Haggai, Zechariah's warning was only received by a remnant (Zech. 8:6, 11, 12, Hag. 1:12, 14, 2:2); therefore, only a few received the blessing, where God would be with them (Hag. 1:13, 2:4b). God was with the remnant because they had considered their ways, repented, and returned to Him.

Jeremiah's message is echoed through Zechariah, "Return to Me, and I will return to you" (Zech. 1:3). The announcement, albeit repeated throughout scripture (for example, Mal. 3:7, Isa. 55:7, Jer. 3:12, 22, Ezek. 33:11, Joel 2:12, etc.) is still a strange notion even for most today. The closest New Testament parallel to Zachariah (Zech. 1:3) is, "Draw near to God, and He will draw near to you" (James. 4:8). However, the same is seen in the letter to the church of Ephesus (Rev. 2:1-7). Note the promise is directly married to the response (Rev. 2:5-7). The exact opposite of the blessing is guaranteed for the one falling (Rev. 2:5b). Like every covenant promise, all promises are and always will be conditional. There is no distinction between the Old Testament and the New with this. For example, Azariah prophesied. "The LORD is with you when you are with Him. If you seek Him, He will be found by you, but if you forsake Him, He will forsake you" (2 Chron. 15:2). Paul suggested something similar, "If we endure, we will also reign with Him; if we deny Him, He will also deny us; if we are faithless, He remains faithful, for He cannot deny Himself" (2 Tim. 2:13).

The call to "Return" (Zech. 1:3) fell on deaf ears for Judah's forefathers (Jer. Jer. 3:12, 14, 22; 4:1, etc.), which is why the call to return follows the statement, "God was very angry" (Zech. 1:2). The call to "Return to Me" is also seen throughout five of the seven letters written to the churches in the book of Revelation (Rev. 2-3). Today, like then, most focus on God's love, kindness, favour, mercy, forgiveness, compassion, and gifts. The gifts are the primary thing within charismatic churches. Rarely today is anything ever said about the anger of God, and even less rare are people seen to respond to such a message, despite scripture having much to say on the topic.

Following Adam and Eve's fall and judgement (Gen. 3), the following example of God's disapproval of humanity's actions is with the Flood (Gen. 6-7). Following the Flood, wherever humanity interfered with God's redemptive plan of salvation, He was, and is, invoked to anger (Zech. 1:15). Again, God's wrath, expressed through the prophet Zechariah, is directed at Judah's ancestors for their false preaching and self-seeking (Zech. 1:2, 7:12, 8:14). Like Zechariah, none of the Old Testament prophets hesitated to warn and write about God's wrath, while the false prophets ignored it, even worse, they replaced it. The same is true today.

Interestingly, the warnings recorded throughout scripture of God's anger, are always at a person, or persons and people groups. No reference is given supporting the idea that God is angry at the sin and not the sinner. The idea is said another way, "God loves the sinner yet hates the sin." Under the inspiration of the Holy Spirit, David says otherwise, "God hates all evildoers" (Ps. 5:4-5). The warning is purposed to invoke lasting repentance (Zech. 1:3), unlike Judah's failed fathers (Zech. 1:4, 6b).

Noteworthy, God's displeasure came first to those called to know and follow Him (1 Pet. 4:17). The very people positioned for prosperity (knowing God) became the cause of anger (Jer. 21:5). Like with the benefits of the covenant, the wrath of God is associated with the agreement (Deut. 28, 30:11-20). God's intention, however, is always for salvation; it was then with Judah, and it is now through the church (1 Thess. 5:9).

Despite the many warnings and the knowledge that God does not change (Num. 23:19, Heb. 13:8, Jam. 1:17b), in contradiction to the above-mentioned, the ancient Israelites, and the modern church [still] lay claim to the 'idea' that God will never judge or leave them/us. Prophetic literature and history alone should be enough to convince us otherwise. The fallacy of unconditional salvation, or eternal security, is the cherry-picked fruit of misquoting half verses like, "He will never leave us or forsake us!" (Heb. 13:5b). The doctrine that God will never leave you is in direct contradiction to His Word and Israel's experience. Implied in the verse above (Heb. 13:5b) and others (cf. 2 Tim. 2:13) is that God is faithful to do what He said He would do, and should you fail to respond accordingly, His Word will overtake you (Zech. 1:6). It is accurate to say, however, that God will never turn back or leave the one holding onto Him - but that one can still turn back from God in the same way a man can break the covenant with his wife or visa-versa.

Again, the idea that God will NEVER leave you falsely stems from cherry-picking verses out of context. Regarding Hebrews (Heb. 13:5), in context, the writer, under the inspiration of the Holy Spirit, instructs the reader to, "Keep your life free from the love of money." In other words, the things of this world can and do take us away from God just as fast and effectively as they did for Judah Iscariot and Demas. The same idea and warning were given by Jesus through Luke's account of the Olivet Discord, stating that the cares of this life could cause you to be left behind, to then endure the tribulation to come (Lu. 21:34-36).

The tribulation to come is also known as the wrath of the Lamb (Rev. 6:16) and the wrath of God (Rev. 14:10), the hour of trial (Rev. 3:10), and the time of vengeance (Jer. 51:6, 2 Thess. 1:8), among other descriptions. Judah's ancestors experienced a shadow of the things to come when exiled from Jerusalem (Lam. 3:5); Jeremiah provides a detailed description of what that experience felt like through the book of Lamentations. Zechariah reminds his audiences of that experience, adding that their forefathers were disqualified (Zech. 1:4, 6), and now they, his hearer, are the subject of the same unless they return and repent. Judah's forefathers experienced a mere shadow of the things to come by comparison. The following judgement of the Jews occurred in 70 A.D. for rejecting Christ. Jews of this generation will experience the final judgement, which will be a time like none other (Jer. 30:7, Dan. 12:1, Matt. 24:21), for the purpose of saving them, even if just a remnant (Rom. 9:27, 11:25-32).

Within the context of Zechariah, the prophet starts by pointing out that although your fathers started on the right foot, with God's favour, they strayed and turned away (Zech. 1:4). Consequently, God became very angry with them (Zech. 1:2). Because Judah's forefathers would not repent and would not return from their wicked ways, God chased them down, despite the claims of the false prophets, "God will not judge us" (Jer. 2:35, cf. 28:10-11). God did judge them, and when He did, they knew it and why (Lam. 1:14, 18, 20, 22). What God said He would do, He did (Lam. 2:17). Through tribulation, God finally got the attention of Judah's forefathers, who then said, "Let us test and examine our ways and return to the Lord" (Lam. 3:40). Zechariah states the same, "So they repented" (Zech. 1:6). However, history and scripture (Zech. 1:4) reveal it was not lasting. Most of the Jews never did turn back to God and or remain; therefore, they perished. What God did to them then, He is about to do again, and like with Judah, even within the tribulation, the prophets and prophetesses will still say, "Mourning I shall never see" (Rev. 18:7b).

Again, Judah's forefathers said God will not judge them, but God did. Zechariah makes a point of this by saying, "Where are they now?" (Zech. 1:5). Fully prepared, confronting, and derailing anticipated liberal replies, the prophet asked three carefully picked and loaded questions: 1). "Where are your fathers now?" 2). "Do they live forever?" (Zech. 1:5), and 3). "Did they [My Words] not overtake your servants?" (Zech. 1:6). Zechariah's warning is direct, intended to disarm and destroy the false covenant security mentality Judah held onto, and with a sense of urgency. Like their forefathers, they did not have unlimited time to respond. Like liberals of every generation, the 'Overtaken' forefathers scoffed at the prophet's warnings, but the question remains, "Where are they now?" And "Did they live forever?" The answer is a resounding, no!

Their opportunity to repent was overtaken and replaced with judgement for Judah's forefathers. The forefathers died in the wilderness by the sword, famine, and pestilences, but God's Word lived on. God's decree, in fact, 'hunted' them down (Zech. 1:6), and now His mercy is granted to another, in their place, like with the church (Rom. 11:17-24). The metaphor, "Overtake you" literally means, "I will hunt, and chase you down," finding its origin in Deuteronomy (Deut. 28:15, 45). Moses' application through the book of Deuteronomy refers to God's curses chasing and catching the evildoer, putting them to death, which is precisely what happened to Israel (Ezek. 37:11).

As mentioned earlier, Zechariah's message to Judah comes five hundred years before Christ; therefore, two thousand, five hundred years ago for us. Yet, the application for us today is still and always will be the same. While many are saying, "Grace, grace" (cf. Zech. 4:7), for the wrong reasons, God is saying, "Repent, repent" (Zech. 1:3, cf. Rev. 2-3). Like Israel and Judah before us, God is affording limited time to return and repent. Paul supports the same by saying, what happened to Israel and Judah serve us as an example, written down for our instruction, on whom the end of the age has come (1 Cor. 10:11). Still, like with Israel and Judah then and now, most do not have ears to hear; most cannot heed the warning. For the same reason, God was angry with Judah then, and He is angry with the rebellious now, hence the wrath to come (Isa. 13:9, Lu. 3:7, 1 Thess. 1:10, 2:16, Rev. 12:12, 19:15).

In the same way, Zechariah's audience thought, "Not me!" God warned them, yes, you, too! Just as it was for your forefathers, it will be for you also; the same applies to the Jews today and to the sleepy, lukewarm church. The next event on the biblical calendar is the fulfilment of the prophecies recorded in Zechariah's book, and the book of Revelation, chapters six to nineteen.

RETURN AND REBUILD

'Obey the Lord'
(Hag. 1-2)

Following an introduction to Zechariah (Zech. 1:1-6), by way of providing further background, it is essential to reference Haggai. As mentioned in the previous section, Haggai was Zechariah's contemporary, bringing the same message, to the same people, at the same time, for the same reason. Like Zechariah, Haggai was an authenticated prophet of God, bringing forth the message of God (Hag. 1:2, 7, 13, 2:4, 6-9, 11, 14, 23). However, Haggai's message was primarily addressing Judah's leaders, often with the introduction, from the "Lord Almighty" (fourteen times). As mentioned in the previous sections, Haggai's message was like that of every other prophet, one of rebuke, with an aim to produce obedience through fear (Hag. 1:12). God's rebuke addressed, "these people" (Hag. 1:2), no longer considered to be His people because they had learned nothing from the exile (Dan. 9:13), therefore had forsaken Him again.

As mentioned in the previous section, after seventy years, Judah was released from captivity by King Cyrus and Darius to rebuild the temple. The time of release correlates with the book of Daniel, chapter nine, where Daniel thought the Messiah was coming to judge the nations and establish His reign from Jerusalem (2 Chron. 36-22-23, Ezra 1:1-11, 2:1-70,

Ps. 126, 147). Again, at the time, Daniel was deeply concerned, knowing Judah had learned nothing (Dan. 9:13). Yet still, God kept to His word and released the exiles after seventy years, resulting in a great celebration (Ezra 3:4-5). Judah sang to the Lord with praise, "He is good" (Ezra 3:11).

Note Psalm 126, "The Lord has done amazing things for us" (v. 3), repeated by Ezra, "He is good!" (Ezra 3:11), compared with Jeremiah's writings in the book of Laminations (Lam. 3:22-26). Even though there was tribulation (Lam. 3:5), God was still good, and although His actions towards Judah were severe, they were just and long overdue. Jeremiah and Ezra's words echoed David's, who compared how God responds to the wicked and the faithful (Ps. 36). God's love is not extended to or experienced by the rebellious other than through grace given to repent and return. Judah experienced both the wrath of God and His love. Severity when fallen, kindness when returning and remaining (cf. Rom. 11:22).

The number of Jews returning to Jerusalem was but a remnant (Ezra 1:4, Hag. 1:14), amounting to 42,360, with an additional number of servants (7,337) and singers (200) (Ezra 2:64). Remember, when King Nebuchadnezzar captured Judah, so many Jews were either killed or captured that the nation was lost. Those deported repopulated, as instructed, during seventy years of captivity (Jer. 28:4-6).

After arriving in Jerusalem in the first year of Darius' reign, the Jews started rebuilding the temple, starting with the alter, and recommencing sacrifices in the Holy Land (Ezra 3:1-6). Following the building of the altar, in the second year of arrival, the Jews began rebuilding the temple (Ezra 3:1-17). Everyone was involved in the project (Ezra 3:8) - yet not all were pleased with the progress when comparing the second temple with the first (Ezra 3:12, Hag. 2:3, Zech. 4:10). Furthermore, not everyone was happy with the project, for the enemies of Judah attempted to interfere with the progress through trickery, bribes, and threats (Ezra 4:1-5). Judah's enemies were victorious for a time, stopping the assignment (Ezra 4:24-5:1). The work stopped until Darius succeeded Cyrus. At that time, the prophets Haggai and Zechariah prophesied to the Jews in Jerusalem (Ezra 5:1).

On the third year back in the Land, Haggai received a word from the Lord, addressing the Jews who claimed, "The time has not yet come to rebuild the house of the Lord" (Hag. 1:2). The temple remained in ruins while the high priests lived in luxury (Hag. 1:1-4, 9). In pursuit of prosperity (Hag. 1:9b), the Jews abandoned God's work in favour of their own, yet to no avail. No matter what they did to fill their pockets, whatever went in, came out just as fast (Hag. 1:5-6). Whatever the Jews could acquire, God blew it away (Hag. 1:9a).

As a side note, I am reminded of a televangelist who recently claimed to be, "Standing in the office of a prophet." He thereby proclaimed to be speaking on behalf of God (thus saith the mighty spirit), commanding that coronavirus to be destroyed, before 'blowing it away.' The 'prophet' finished his performance by saying, "It (coronavirus) is finished; it is gone forever." That spectacle occurred in March 2020. Unlike the false prophets, when God speaks through His prophets, what He says He would do, He does accomplish (Zech. 1:6). The fulfilment of the prophetic word is the test of prophecy, determining the true from the false (Deut. 18:20). Unlike the above-mentioned would-be 'prophet,' when God blew, whatever He blew on was either destroyed or transformed (Jn. 3:8). In Judah's case, Judah's self-seeking labour was destroyed.

Judah's neglect brought God's correction through the prophet, "Consider your ways!" (Hag. 1:5, 7), and, "Rebuild My house!" (Hag. 1:8), which would also be a timely message for the would-be self-proclaiming 'prophet' mentioned above, "Consider your ways, stop building your own house, instead, build mine!"

The phrase, "Consider your ways" (Hag. 1:8) literally means, "Examine yourself" (Hag. 1:7; 2:15, 18 [twice]). God continued to address Judah, promising that if they returned to work and rebuilt the temple, He would prosper them (Hag. 1:8b). The promise of prosperity was conditional on Judah's obedience (Hag. 1:12-15, 2:10-19). The primary point of prosperity is to again be with God and thus have God with them (Hag. 1:13, 2:4-5). However, God would not be with them until they first, "Considered their ways," repented, and returned (Zech. 1:3) through fear and lasting obedience (Hag. 1:12-13). Lasting obedience, beginning with rebuilding the house of God (Hag. 1:14).

Now that God's people were back where they ought to be, with God, the prophet Haggai asked three questions, 1). Who is left among you who saw this house in its former glory?" (Hag. 2:3); 2). How do you see it now?" (Hag. 2:3), and 3). "Is it not as nothing in your eyes?" (Hag. 2:4). As mentioned earlier, those who remembered the former temple were not in the least bit impressed with the new. But the word was to them, "Be strong (three times) and get to work" (Hag. 2:4). Interestingly, David used the exact words with the building of the first temple (1 Chron. 28:10, 20). Haggai added to his message, "Do not be afraid" (Hag. 2:5), "The future glory of this temple will be greater than its past glory" (Hag. 2:9).

The future glory of the temple follows God shaking the nations (Hag. 2:7), "In a little while" (Hag. 2:6), where everything that is His would be returned to Him, being absolutely everything because absolutely everything belongs to God (Hag. 2:8). Here, the prophet leaps from the second temple to the millennial temple some two thousand, five hundred years into the future, yet states the prophecy would be fulfilled, "In a little while" (Hag. 2:6). By comparison to eternity, and the time remaining until the end of the age, two thousand, five hundred years may seem short to God. But before the millennium, a time of shaking comes first, referring to the tribulation at the close of this age, preparing for the next (Matt. 24:29, Heb. 12:26, Rev. 6:12-13, 8:12). The following age, being the millennium, or the seventh day, is the next dispensation where the last and millennial temple will exist. Alongside Haggai, Zechariah also speaks of the last temple in chapters six and eight, with additional references in chapter fourteen.

Before the millennial temple, the third tribulation temple is still yet to be built. Paul narrows in on the third temple (2 Thess. 2:4), as did Jesus (Matt. 24:15), quoting Daniel (Dan. 9:27, 11:31). Jesus provided John with more information on the third temple, recorded in the book of Revelation (Rev. 11). The next temple will be built during the tribulation; materials have already been secured, and Levitical training is ongoing in preparation for the sacrifices. The only thing needed is the location where the Dome on the Rock currently stands. The prediction is, sometime soon, in a little while, the Dome on the Rock will fall, perhaps due to an earthquake, and then be replaced by the third temple. Jerusalem is on a Faultline; therefore, the theory of an earthquake destroying the Dome on the Rock is entirely plausible.

Furthermore, it is prophesied that Israel will experience some significant earthquakes during the tribulation (Ezek. 38:19, Zech. 14:15, Rev. 11:13, 19); however, these are reserved for the midway point of the seven-year ordeal. Adding further support to the argument, the earthquake following the raptured witnesses (Rev. 11:12-13) could be a repeat of another when the church is removed (Rev. 4:1). When the church is taken or snatched away, graves will open, and the dead will rise (1 Thess. 4:16) in the same way they did when Christ was resurrected (Matt. 27:52). Around that same time, there was a great earthquake (Matt. 28:2); therefore, it is reasoned that the same will occur with the church's rapture, like with the two witnesses (Rev. 11:12-13) destroying the Dome on the Rock. Rabbis predict that the third temple will take two years to complete once the location is available

The temple project will begin at the beginning of the tribulation and be complete before the midpoint. This will allow the antichrist to take his seat and announce that he is God (2 Thess. 2:4). By signing the seven-year peace treaty (Isa. 28:15, 18, Dan. 9:24-27), the antichrist is revealed, and then again by standing in the temple announcing that he is God (Dan. 7:25, 11:36, Matt. 24:15, Rev. 13:5-6). He is also revealed by forcing everyone, small and great, to receive his mark (Rev. 13:18).

The antichrist is the white rider released at the tribulation's commencement with the breaking of the first seal (Rev. 6:2). Zechariah has two visions of the four apocalyptic horsemen, who the antichrist is among (Zech. 1:7-17, 6:1-8). The antichrist (counterfeit Christ) goes about deceiving and conquering (killing) those left behind (those who missed the rapture). He is the strong delusion, the deceiver, who God sends to those refusing to love the truth, that they may believe what is false, and be condemned (2 Thess. 2:10-12). And condemned, they will be (Rev. 14:9-11, 16:2, 19:20, cf. 20:4).

In a little while (Hag. 2:6), God will shake the heavens and the earth and the sea and the drylands when the antichrist is released God will also shake the nations (Hag. 2:6-7). Again, the shaking speaks first of an earthquake, or earthquakes. During the tribulation, earthquakes will be a global event (Rev. 6:12, 8:5, 16:18), indicating that God is very angry (Isa. 13:13. Rev. 6:16). After the tribulation, when Jesus returns (Matt. 24:29), He will again shake the nations, returning to Him everything that is His (Hag. 2:8). He will also, "Fill this (His) house (the temple) with glory" (Hag. 2:7). To reiterate, the house referred to is the millennial temple, not the tribulation temple. It is predicted the earthquake accompanying Jesus' return will destroy the third temple, making room for the next.

When Jesus returns and shakes the nations, He provides refuge for those trusting in Him (Joel 3:16), even affording one last opportunity for anyone to submit (Zech. 12:10). The only thing surviving the shaking to come will be the kingdom of God and those who are in it (Heb. 12:28).

Through the shaking, in the same way, the wealth of Israel was offered up for the rebuilding of the second temple (Ezra 1:4-6, 9-11). The wealth of the nations will be repossessed for the building of the last (Hag. 2:8, Zech. 14:14). Again, on completion, the last temple will be filled with the glory of God, not because of worldly wealth, but because God is there. Today, many talk about the glory of God being greater in the latter days than the former (Hag. 2:9), claiming for themselves revival. That nonsense is on par with another useless saying, "The best is yet before us." Isaiah answers that delusion, calling the duped "Dumb dogs" (Isa. 56:10-11). Isaiah's rebuke refers to Israel's leaders who refused to warn God's people of the things to come and that they would repent. Instead, they filled them with false prophecies, dreams, and visions while filling their stomachs, and pockets with whatever they could get their hands on.

In no way does the glory of God, to come, refer to anything liberal preachers claim, but rather God's very presence in His house repeating that of old (Ex. 40:34–35; 1 Kgs. 8:10–11), which follows the tribulation shaking. Ezekiel provides some description of the future temple and the glory of God, where the Lord will fill the temple, and Israel will no longer be defiled (Ezek. 43:1-12). At that time, in the millennium, there will be lasting peace (Hag. 2:9). Jesus, the Prince of Peace (Isa. 9:6), is ruling from the temple with an iron rod (Rev. 2:27, 19:15). No more will the nations rage (Ps. 2), and neither will the charlatan ever trouble God's people again with false prophecies (Zech. 13:2-6). Clearly, these prophecies are still yet to be fulfilled.

Haggai's message to Judah, two thousand, five hundred years ago, is as relevant for us today. The prophet confronted the backslidden nation, motivating them to repent and obey through fear (Hag. 1:12), as did Zechariah (Zech. 1:2, 4-6), to get them back on track, "Return, obey and rebuild." By rebuking Judah's leaders, the prophet brought the nation back on track and encouraged them to look beyond the present towards the coming Messiah and His established rule and reign in the Millennium.

Also seen through this section of scripture is that God is not so much interested in what we can build for ourselves or for Him, but rather in our hearts. When Judah's elders revealed their disappointment with the second temple by comparison to the first, the prophet encouraged them to look beyond it. God was not concerned about how it looked on the outside, for He will fill it with His glory. The same is true for us, as the temple of God (1 Cor. 6:19-20). Our job is only to be that temple by coming to and remaining in Christ Jesus, watching for Him, thereby being found ready when He returns. By doing so, God will fill that temple with His Holy Spirit.

SEEK FIRST THE KINGDOM

'The Coming Glory'
(Hag. 2:10-23)

As mentioned previously, it was in the second year of King Darius's reign that Zechariah prophesied to Judah (Zech. 1:1), saying, "I the Lord, was very angry with your ancestors" (Zech. 1:2), followed by, "Return to Me and I will return to you" (Zech. 1:3). In the same year, God sent the prophet Haggai with his third message (Hag. 2:10). The first message instructed the Jews to rebuild the temple (Hag. 1). The second message revealed the future glory of the temple (Hag. 2:1-9). Now the third reiterates God's blessing that follows obedience (Hag. 2:10-19).

Zechariah reminded the Jews of what He did to their forefathers, saying that if they did the same thing, they would be treated in the same way (Zech. 1:4-6). In short, disobedience brings the curse (Deut. 28:15-68). Haggai takes it further, stating obedience brings blessing (Deut. 28:1-14). Zechariah picks up on the same from chapter two (vv. 1-5). As seen through the chapters in the book of Deuteronomy, God, through Moses, repeats this universal and divine nature of blessings and curses, life, and death (Deut. 30:11-20).

Blessings and curses follow the Law. Where the Law is kept, blessings flow. Where the Law is broken, curses follow. For this reason, God sent

Haggai to address Judah, asking about the Law, "What does the Law say? (Hag. 2:11). In other words, "What is your priestly position?" The prophet inquired about carrying holy meat in a garment (Hag. 2:12) and encountering the dead (Hag. 2:13). In sum, God asked the priests, if something holy touches another item, will the thing also become holy? No! If someone touches something unclean and then handles anything else, it will become contaminated. Yes. Then, so it is with a nation in disobedience (Hag. 2:14). Judah's sacrificial worship was defiled due to sinning.

The prophet's rebuke brought about change, following the words, "Consider your ways" (Hag. 2:15). Haggai used the phrase before (cf. Hag. 1:5, 7), repeating it (Hag. 2:15, 18 [twice]), which, again, means, "Examine yourself" (2 Cor. 13:5). Paul used the phrase, "Examine yourself" to test whether you are in the faith. Haggai's reference points back to the consequence of sin, being poverty (Hag. 1:6, 9). Because of sin, God blew on Judah's labors. God blowing on Judah's crop refers to disease (Hag. 2:17, cf. Amos 4:9) and hail (cf. Ex. 9:25). The prophet Amos states that God destroyed Israel's crop because they did not return to Him (Amos 4:9); that is, they did not turn from their sin, repeating the sins of their forefathers.

The remainder of Israel's past failures, and consequences, serve to position the current generation for blessing. God wants to bless His people! Remember and renew; consider what you do (Hag. 1:5, 7, 2:15, 18). Again, Haggai addressed Judah's disobedience (Hag. 1:4-9), resulting in drought (Hag. 1:10-11), now saying, obedience brings blessing (Hag. 2:19).

On the condition that Judah repents, returns, and remains, God promised them, "From this day on I will bless you" (Hag. 2:19). The evidence of Judah's repentance starts with rebuilding the temple, which they did (Ezra 5:2) after considering their ways. It was also "On that same day" (Hag. 2:20) God sent the fourth message through the prophet Haggai that He (God) was, "About to shake the heavens and the earth and overthrow the chariots and their riders. And the horses and the riders shall go down, everyone by the sword of his brother" (Hag. 2:21-22). The prophet continues, "On that day, declares the LORD of hosts, I will take you, O Zerubbabel my servant, the son of Shealtiel, declares the LORD, and make you like a signet ring, for I have chosen you, declares the LORD of hosts" (Hag. 2:23).

On a day, in the future, "In a little while," God will, "shake the heavens and the earth" (Hag. 2:6-7, 21). As mentioned in the previous section, the shaking speaks of an earthquake directed at the Gentile nations (cf. Zech. 1:15). After the tribulation, God will overthrow the Gentile kingdoms of nations (Hag. 2:22) that have been and are trampling Jerusalem underfoot (Ps. 79:1, Isa. 68:3, 18, Dan. 8:13, Zech. 12:3, Lu. 21:24, Rev. 11:2).

Haggai's prophesy repeats Daniel's (Dan. 2, 7), where the Messianic kingdom will replace the Gentile kingdom following the war. In war (the red horse, Rev. 6:3-4) the Gentile nations will be overthrown by the sword (Hag. 2:22), which will be fulfilled at the battle of Armageddon (Rev. 16:16-18). When Jesus Returns (Rev. 19:11–21), many will turn against his own brother with the sword (cf. Zech. 12:2–9; 14:1–5).

Following the pronouncement of future blessing, being the restoration of Israel, Haggai continues to encourage Zerubbabel. "On that day" (Hag. 2:23a), God would take and make him like a signet ring (Hag. 2:23b). The signet ring represents authority, suggesting Zerubbabel would have authority in the millennial dispensation, such as a restored son (Lu. 15:22). Unlike Judah's ancestors from whom God tore off the signet ring (Jer. 22:24), it would remain on Zerubbabel's hand.

CHAPTER ONE—PART TWO

THE HORSEMAN

'Cry Out—Seek the Kingdom'
(Zech. 1:7-17)

Three Months On - (from Zech. 1:1-6). Two-three months after Haggai brought his third (Hag. 2:10-19) and fourth (Hag. 2:20-23) message promising blessing for obedience, Zechariah received another message from the Lord (Zech. 1:7), this time through a vision (Zech. 1:8). The vision of the horseman is the first of eight. The vision came five months after the Jews got back to work, rebuilding the temple (Hag. 1:14-15, 2:15).

Previously, the prophet was calling God's people to return, repent and rebuild. Three months later, the prophet received a vision bringing hope for Israel, picking up from where Haggai left off. Haggai concluded his short book by prophesying the destruction of the Gentile nations (Hag. 2:6-7, 20-22) and the establishment of the millennial kingdom (Hag. 2:23). The millennial kingdom is the time of Israel's future hope, following the judgement of every other earthly kingdom (Zech. 1:15).

Zechariah's vision consists of what was seen (Zech. 1:8), accompanied by an explanation (Zech. 1:9-11) and intercession (Zech. 1:12-17). The vision focuses on four horse riders, narrowing in on the red horse (war, cf. Rev. 6:3-4). Verse eight introduces a man whom God has sent riding on a red horse, patrolling the earth (Zech. 1:10b). The leader of the horsemen is called, "The angel of the Lord" (Zech. 1:11). The rider is in the company of three others behind him (Zech. 1:8b), another reddish-brown, then sorrel (brown), and white (Zech. 1:8). The riders report that the earth remains at rest (Zech. 1:11). The fact that the whole earth is referenced suggests the focus is much bigger than just Jerusalem, confirmed by verse fifteen.

Like Daniel, Zechariah had difficulty understanding the visions, often responding with the words, "What are these?" (Zech. 1:9, cf. 1:19; 4:4, 11; 6:4; also cf. 5:6). Also, as with Daniel and angel answers. On occasion, the angel even pre-empts the conversation by asking the prophet, "What do you see?" or "What do you know?" (Zech. 4:2, 5, 13; 5:2). On each occasion, the angel who was talking with Zechariah (1:11, 13–14, 19; 2:3; 4:1, 4–5; 5:10; 6:4), was not the same as the "Angel of the Lord" (Zech. 1:11-12, 3:1-6). The angel of the Lord speaks on behalf of the other riders whom God has sent to patrol the earth (Zech. 1:10). The 'patrolling' is military surveillance of world governments.

After patrolling the globe, the angels report to the angel of the Lord that all the earth remains at rest (Zech. 1:11). However, the report conflicts with the following statement, "Will you have no mercy on Jerusalem?" (Zech. 1:12), not to mention verse fifteen, where God is said to be exceedingly angry with the nations, "That are at ease." The term, 'at ease', refers to being proud (Ps. 132:4). Perhaps the 'ease' of the nations is also that of, "Peace and security" (1 Thess. 5:3) and being deeply opposed to God (Zech. 1:14-15). Either way, the nations 'at ease' are up to no good, ultimately resulting in terror, first and temporality for Israel, scattering the

Jews across the globe (Zech. 1:21), and then for themselves (Zech. 1:15, 21) when God judges the nations.

Amidst great and global trouble, verses fourteen to seventeen reveal that God is still and always will be in control. He is all-knowing and very present, watching, overseeing, and orchestrating the various events. Verse thirteen also reveals God's everlasting love for Israel with gracious and comforting words, "Cry out, thus says the LORD of hosts: I am exceedingly jealous for Jerusalem and Zion. And I am exceedingly angry with the nations that are at ease; for while I was angry but a little, they furthered the disaster. Therefore, thus says the LORD, I have returned to Jerusalem with mercy: my house shall be built in it, declares the LORD of hosts, and the measuring line shall be stretched out over Jerusalem. Cry out again, thus says the LORD of hosts: My cities shall again, overflow with prosperity, and the LORD will again comfort Zion and again choose Jerusalem" (Zech. 1:15-17).

Again, the message communicates God's love for Israel (Zech. 1:13–14), His anger on the nations (Zech. 1:15), and the promise of prosperity in Israel (Zech. 1:16–17). Clearly, the prophecy is yet to be fulfilled, and soon will be, following the intense persecution of Israel (Isa. 28:14-15, 18, 22, Jer. 30:7, Dan. 12:1, Matt. 24:9-22, Rev. 12:13-16). However, in that time of tribulation, God will protect the Jews (Zech. 8:2, Rev. 12). God was angry with Judah for seventy years (Zech. 1:12, cf. 1:2), and now, He is very angry with the nations (Zech. 1:15), further revealed in the second vision (Zech. 1:18-21). After seven years of tribulation, God will execute judgement on the Gentile nations and fully restore Israel.

Israel will be fully restored in the millennial kingdom, where God promises six blessings:

1. God has returned to Israel with mercy (Zech. 1:16a)
2. God will build His house (Zech. 1:16b)

3. God will rebuild the city of Jerusalem (Zech. 1:17a)
4. Jerusalem will overflow with wealth (Zech. 1:17b)
5. Jerusalem will be comforted by God (Zech. 1:17c)
6. Jerusalem will be chosen by God (Zech. 1:17d)

Again, the blessings promised to Israel are reserved for when Christ returns and sets up His rule and reign on the earth. Any suggestion of the church inheriting the said blessings (replacement theology) is poor scholarship at best. The promise refers to Israel's inheritance, for whom God was angry; they will return to Him and be saved through the coming tribulation (Matt. 23:39) and then restored in the millennium (Rom. 11:26-27). The church will also inherit her own rewards in the millennial, not before.

At the time of Zechariah's writings, the second temple was being rebuilt and was completed around four years later (Ezra 6:15). The divine glory of God never returned to the second temple and will not return until the millennial temple comes down from heaven to the earth (Zech. 1:16, cf. Ezek. 10:18–19; 11:22–23). Nevertheless, the Jews looked to the promise, expecting it to be fulfilled in their day, in "A little while" (Hag. 2:6). Before the glory does return, they will be scattered once more (Zech. 1:18-21).

In conclusion, the shaking of the nations, as mentioned above, takes place during the coming tribulation (Rev. 6-19). During that time, the Jews will be scattered, and then, they will, "Call on the Name of the Lord" (Matt. 23:39), resulting in the greatest of revivals the world has ever seen (Rev. 7), yet not without unprecedented trouble (Jer. 30:7, Matt 24:21). Following the worst persecution, the Jews have ever seen, "From this day" (Hag. 2:19) they will be restored (Zech. 1:17). Then, in the millennial, peace and prosperity will overflow throughout Jerusalem. God will return to the Jews; they will again be chosen and comforted by Jesus, whom they have not known.

Once the vision was given, the prophet was to 1). "Cry out," and encourage Israel (Zech. 1:14, 17), return, and remain (Zech. 1:3); and 2). To, "Cry out" and encourage them (Zech. 1:17). In sum, the future is bright for those seeking God's kingdom first, and conversely, the future is grim for those who do not. Yet still, before the blessing, great tribulation comes first (Jer. 30:7, Dan. 12:1, Matt. 24:21).

CHAPTER ONE—PART THREE

FOUR HORNS / FOUR CRAFTSMEN

'The Nations that are at Rest'
(Zech. 1:18-21)

Following the previous section, where the patrolling angels reported, "The earth remains at rest" (Zech. 1:11) comes the continuation of the first vision (Zech. 1:8, 18), where the prophet saw the future judgement of the Gentile kingdoms (Zech. 1:18-21). Remember, God is, "Exceedingly angry with the nations that are at ease" (Zech. 1:15, cf. v. 11). God is angry with the nations who are at ease for three reasons: 1). They have contributed to Israel's troubles (Zech. 1:19-21); 2). They have done nothing to help Israel in a time of trouble (Matt. 25:41-46); 3). They are so consumed with worldliness, false peace, and prosperity that God has been removed from their radar (Jer. 51, Rev. 18). Again, for this reason, "In a little while," God will shake them (Hag. 2:7-8, 21); that is, He will, "Destroy the strength of the kingdoms of the nations" (Hag. 2:22). When God shakes the nations, the very things they pursued in replacement of

Him will be taken from them, "The silver is mine, and the gold is mine, declares the Lord of Hosts" (Hag. 2:8).

As a side note, the proclamation, the silver, and the gold belong to God is a good reminder for prosperity preachers who peddle and pimp the gospel for greedy gain. As seen throughout the book of Zechariah and Haggai, nations are not the only ones guilty of loving money. Remember, God judged Judah by striking all their products of their toil with blight, mildew, and hail due to their faithlessness - and even then, they did not return to Him (Hag. 2:17). For all their labors, they reaped nothing, likened to having holes in their pockets (Hag. 1:6), because God blew their works away (Hag. 1:9). The prosperity problem is seen again in Zechariah's book, where the former prophets of Jerusalem, enjoying prosperity (Zech. 7:7), were judged because they refused to listen to God and even prevented others from hearing Him (Zech. 7:11-12) - therefore, God scattered Judah among all the nations (Zech. 7:13).

The issues for Judah's ancestors were a lack of kindness and mercy (Zech. 7:8). There is also a lack of loving and sharing, particularly with the most vulnerable. The former prophets oppressed the widow, the fatherless, the stranger, and the poor (Zech. 7:10). Going further again, they devised evil against one another in their hearts (Zech. 7:10) and then, "Made their heart diamond-hard, lest they should hear the law and the words that the Lord of hosts had sent by His Spirit through the former prophets" (Zech. 7:12a). For this reason, "Great anger came from the Lord of host" (Zech. 7:12b). As mentioned before, God does not change (Nu. 23:19, Heb. 13:8, Ja. 1:17), a warning which serves those tempted to merchandise God and the people of God.

The same sins of Judah have been repeated by the church, as addressed by Jesus through the letters to the churches, in particular, Sardis and Laodicea (Rev. 3:1-6, 14-22). The church of Sardis had a reputation of being alive but was dead, and the church of Laodicea had everything and no need for anything, apparently! The latter serves as the best example that scripture provides of a prosperity-driven church. However, both were in grave danger, the danger of judgement unless repentance came first and fast. While the letters to the churches (Rev. 2-3) addressed literal churches at the time of writing (95 A.D), the message to each is timeless and prophetic, explicitly addressing the last (lukewarm) twenty-first-century church before Jesus returns (Rev. 3:14-22) by way of the rapture (Rev. 3:10, 4:1, cf. Lu. 21:34-36, Rom. 5:9, 1 Cor. 15:51-52, 1 Thess. 4:16-17, 1 Thess. 5:9, 2 Thess. 2:7, Tit. 2:13).

Paul warned before Jesus returns for His church, the love of money (within the church) will increase (2 Tim. 3:1-2). The love of money increasing within the church is indirectly seen when Paul says, "For the time will come when men will not tolerate sound doctrine, but with itching ears, they will gather around themselves teachers to suit their own desires. So, they will turn their ears away from the truth and turn aside to myths" (2 Tim. 4:3-4). Myths include the wealth, health, and happiness 'gospel' (God wants you to be rich, overflowing in everything, lacking nothing) promoted by charismatic churches. Previously, Paul said, "The love of money is the root of all kinds of evil" (1 Tim. 6:10). For Judah's ancestors the love of money caused them to forget and oppress the widow, the fatherless, the stranger, and the poor. At the time of Haggai and Zechariah, materialism caused Judah to forget God and seek their own interests. Again, the same is particularly true for the churches, Sardis, Laodicea, and modern-day types. The nations have also forgotten God, whom He is about to shake (cf. Heb. 12:25-27). "In a little while" (Hag. 2:6), when God shakes the nations, only those within the kingdom will remain (Heb. 12:28). Soon, "While people are saying peace and security, then sudden destruction will come upon them as labor pains come upon a pregnant woman, and they will not escape" (1 Thess. 5:3).

While the nations remain at rest (Zech. 1:11) and are at ease (Zech. 1:15), the prophet is called to, "Cry out" (Zech. 1:14), God loves you, Israel, "Cry out," "I (God) am about to prosper Jerusalem" (Zech. 1:17). Jerusalem's prosperity results from the redistribution of wealth (Hag. 2:7-8), where God will take the wealth of the sinner and give it to the just man (Prov. 13:22). The promise is extended to those who return to God and remain in Him. As mentioned in the previous section, the promise of prosperity is fulfilled in the millennial dispensation following Christ's return (Rev. 5:10, 11:15). At the second coming of Jesus Christ, the nations will be shaken and judged, which Zechariah saw when writing about the four horns (Zech. 1:18-21).

The four horns symbolise kingdoms (Dan. 2, 7, 8:3, Rev. 17:12). If the horns are the same that Daniel saw, as some suggest, they will represent Medo-Persia, Greece, Rome, and the Messianic kingdom. However, the fourth kingdom will not be shaken; therefore, the assumption is flawed (cf. Dan. 2, 7). Further supporting Daniel, chapters two and seven is chapter eight, which also references horns, symbolic of powers and kingdom. The two kingdoms are 1). Media, Persia, and 2). Greece (Dan. 8:20-21). Greece succeeded Medo-Persia and then was followed by Rome. Rome started losing its power in 395 A.D and finally fell in 476 A.D. Therefore, the horns do not apply to the pre-existing ruling nations but rather nations existing when Christ returns. The top four superpowers today are:

7. The United States of America
8. China
9. The European Union
10. Russia

They of the top four superpowers listed above are also referenced as end-times players, China (Dan. 11:40-45, Rev. 9:13-19, 16:12-16, cf. Joel 2), Russia (Ezek. 38-39, Dan. 11:40-45), and the Revived Roman Empire (Europe), (Dan. 2:40-44, 7:7, 20, 24, Rev. 12:3, 13:1, 17:3, 7, 12, 16). The USA is not mentioned in scripture and is therefore unlikely to be among the said horns due to the scattering and terrifying of Israel (Zech. 1:21). The USA is Israel's ally and greatest defender. When Israel is attacked during the tribulation, there will be none (of any significance) to help her, so they need to flee (Matt. 24:15, Rev. 12, cf. Isa. 26:20-21, Dan. 12:1b. Zeph. 2:3). Therefore, the USA is either no longer Israel's ally, or they are incapable of defending her.

However, Egypt and the kings of the south represent a Middle Eastern army, making a fourth horn (Dan. 11:40-43, cf. Isa. 17, Ps. 83). All four horns will want Israel's natural recourses being land, oil, and gas. The Revived Roman Empire (Europe), consisting of ten horns (Rev. 12:3, 13:1, 17:3, 7, 12, 16), will be chief, killing tens of thousands of the Jews in their homeland (Dan. 11:41). The European army is led by the antichrist (Rev. 17:10-14). Russia and China will attack the antichrist from the midpoint of the tribulation, invading Jerusalem (Dan. 11:40-45). Finally, the armies of the antichrist, the east, and the north will gather at Megiddo for the battle of Armageddon (Rev. 16:16). On that day, Jesus will return, destroy the invading armies, and the armies of the antichrist (Zech. 10—14, Rev. 17:12-14.19:11-18, 21), before setting up His own kingdom.

After the tribulation, all four end times superpowers that trouble Israel will themselves be struck with a heavy blow (craftsman/blacksmith, Zech. 1:20). The horns that scattered Israel will be smashed with the blow of a blacksmith (cf. Dan. 2:33-34, 40-45). Interestingly, the prophet Hosea uses the word 'Craftsmen', charging Israel with the sin of idolatry, saying, "And now they sin more and more, and make for themselves metal images, idols skillfully made of their silver, all of them the work of craftsmen." It is said of them, "Those who offer human sacrifice kiss calves!" (Hos. 13:2). Hosea was the last prophet to address Israel before the kingdom fell to Assyria (around 722 B.C). God instructed the prophet to marry a prostitute to illustrate Israel's whoredom, warning punishment would come if they did not return to Him. Judgement did come, just as predicted (Hos. 5:15), causing Israel to return (Hos. 6:1).

God punished Israel and then Judah. Now, through the prophet Zechariah, He is threatening to do the same again to Judah's offspring (Zech. 1-6) and prophesying the future punishment of the four horns (nations) that also commit idolatry (cf. Hag. 2:7-8). Only this time, with Zechariah's prophecy, instead of the craftsmen acquiring wealth, they destroy it (Zech. 1:18, 20). Unlike Hosea's reference, the craftsmen in Zechariah's prophecy are angels. After the tribulation, four angels strike the four horns.

The book of Revelation reveals that there will be two groups of four angels (Rev. 7:1, 2, & 9:14, 15). The first group was given the power to harm the earth and sea (Rev. 7:2), and the second was given the authority to kill one-third of humanity (Rev. 9:15). John's revelation has some interesting similarities with the four horses (angels) of Zechariah's visions (Zech. 1:7-17) and four chariots (Zech. 6:1-8). While John saw four angels hold back the winds (Rev. 7:1), Zechariah saw four winds (angels) who, like the four horses (Zech. 1:10), patrol the earth (Zech. 6:7). The latter refers to divine judgement (Jer. 49:36; Dan. 7:2; Rev. 7:1).

Zechariah's eighth vision of the four chariots (Zech. 6:1-8) suggests this event occurs at the end of the tribulation. As recorded in Ezekiel, the words, "My Spirit" (Zech. 6:8) arguably refer to God's wrath subsiding. During the tribulation, God's wrath, is shifted to Babylon after being poured out on the wicked, (Zech. 5:5–11; cf. Rev. 18:2, 10, 21; 19:1–3). Once the wrath of God is dispensed (Rev. 6:16, 14:10, 16:17) and is satisfied (Rev.

15:1, 16:17), then His Spirit will come to rest. In the first vision, God was angry with the nations who felt secure in their arrogance and pride (Zech. 1:15). In the eighth vision, He was content with their just judgement (cf. Rev. 19:2, 15-19), which is what the nations deserved (Rev. 16:6).

The passages in (Zech. 1:18-21) reveal that God will raise the four horns to scatter Israel and then send four blacksmiths as His instrument of judgement. God judges Israel and then the nations. After, and throughout the judgement, worse than ever seen before (Jer. 30:7, Dan. 12:1, Matt. 24:21), God delivers His people (cf. Isa. 26:10). The deliverance and salvation of God's people prepare them for the Messianic kingdom, where all the promises of peace and prosperity are fulfilled. Then, "The latter glory of the house (temple) shall be greater than the former" (Hag. 2:9).

Jeremiah's prophecy (51:20-26) picks up on the same event where Babylon will be used by God, like a war club used to shatter other nations (cf. Isa. 34:1-10). Babylon symbolically refers to the antichrist's kingdom during the tribulation (Rev. 17, 18). During the time of trouble, the armies of the antichrist will shatter the nations (Jer. 51:20-23 x9). The word 'Shatter' is used nine times, indicating the severity of the blow, meaning 'shatter to bits'. After Babylon has shattered the nations, God will shatter her, specifically for her part in troubling Israel and the saints (Rev. 17:5-6, 18:4-6, 24). In the same way, Babylon ruined the nations; God will destroy her in a single day (Rev. 18:8), in a single hour (Rev. 18:10, 17, 19), she will be "No more" (Rev. 18:21, 22 x3, 23 x2, cf. Jer. 51:44, 49, 55). God will destroy the last kingdom and replace it with His own (Dan. 2:40-45, 7:23-27). There will be nothing left of the final earthly kingdom when He does, for her ruins will lie desolate forever (Jer. 51:26, 29, 60-62).

In conclusion, return to Me (Israel), and (then) I (God) will return to you (Isa. 55:7, Jer. 3:12, Ezek. 33:11, Zech. 1:3, cf. Hos. 5:15, 6:1, Mal. 3:7) is the message, then, and now. Although the book of Zechariah addresses Judah, like Hosea addressed Israel, and still does, the church should also take note (cf. Ja. 4:8 Rev. 2:4-5). If the church does what Israel did, it will be treated the same way (cf. Rom. 11:22), evident enough with the five failing churches (Rev. 2-3).

Following the judgement of the church (1 Pet. 4:17), determining who gets taken, or left behind, then Israel is judged in the tribulation. After the trial, the nations are judged (Hag. 2:21-22). Once God's, "Spirit is at rest" (Zech. 6:8), satisfied with the executed judgement, then peace and prosperity will flow (Hag. 2:19, 23). The nations that submit to God and join themselves to Israel during the tribulation (cf. Isa. 26:10) shall become God's people, and God will dwell in their midst during the millennium (Zech. 2:11, 8:3). Those that fail and or refuse to repent during the time of trouble shall be destroyed, struck by the hammer of God (Jer. 51:20-23). Once God has executed judgement on the nations and set up His millennial kingdom, then His people will be at rest, and not before.

CHAPTER TWO

THE MEASURING LINE

'I Will Dwell in Your Midst'
(Zech. 2:1-13)

Continuing from the previous vision of the red rider, symbolising war (Zech. 1:15, 2:8-9, cf. Rev. 6:4), transiting into the next, the prophet "Lifted his eyes" (Zech. 2:1). He received further information and revelation, first for himself (Zech. 2:4-5), then for Israel (Zech. 2:6-12), and the rest of the world (Zech. 2:8, 11, 13, cf. 1:11, 15). Effectively, chapter two of Zechariah's book is a continuation of chapter one, where the opening words still apply, "Return to Me and (then) I will return to you" (Zech. 1:3). The evidence of the statement is seen in verse five, "I will be the glory in her midst," again in verse ten, "I will come and dwell in your midst." Verse eleven repeats verse ten, "I will dwell in your midst," as does verse twelve, "I will dwell in your midst." The big idea of chapter two, following chapter one, is that God will dwell with those (alone) who seek to dwell with Him by returning to Him (Zech. 1:3), by knowing Him (cf. Jer. 9:24, 31:24), and by obeying His commands (cf. Deut. 28). Likewise, the threat (Zech. 1:4-6) is also true for Zechariah's hearers, and every other generation up until Jesus returns, "If you forsake Me, I will forsake you" (2 Chron. 15:2, cf. 2 Tim. 2:11-13).

The promise, as mentioned above, of God dwelling with His people, who seek to dwell with Him, was as actual for Israel as it is for the church and will be for those left behind in the tribulation. As mentioned previously, God, through the prophet Zechariah, leaps two-thousand, five hundred years into the future. Therefore, the prophecy applies to every generation from the time of writing until now. Particularly now, as the fulfilment of the prophecy will be seen and experienced by this generation, the same age who saw Israel reborn in 1948 (cf. Matt. 24:32-35).

Suppose the prediction of that same generation that saw Israel rebirthed would also see the fulfilment of Zechariah's prophecy occurring during the tribulation is correct. In that case, then the time of trouble is at the door therefore the urgency of the message is even more, "Return to Me!" (Zech. 1:3). The urgency of the message was expressed through the prophet at the time of writing, "Run" (Zech. 2:4), "Up, up" (Zech. 2:6), "Up, escape" (Zech. 2:7), and Haggai, "In a little while I will shake the nations" (Hag. 2:6).

When Judah returned to Jerusalem, God sent an angel to measure her borders (Zech. 1:16, 2:1), width, and length (Zech. 2:2); once done, the command was to "Run…, Jerusalem shall be inhabited" (Zech. 2:4). On completion of the prophecy, Jerusalem will not need walls due to being protected by a wall of fire (Zech. 2:5a). The wall of fire is directly related to Jesus' dwelling in the city, the One whose glory fills it (Zech. 2:5b). On the grounds that Jerusalem is still troubled by its neighbors, lacking the protective wall of fire and the presence of God, the prophesy is still to be fulfilled. Around five hundred and fifty years after the Jews returned to the holy land, they were scattered again in 70 A.D. After seventy years in captivity, they remained scattered until 1948.

When Israel was reborn, her borders were determined by the British mandate on Palestine. Also, on the outcome of the Israeli War of Independence of 1948-1949, and again with the consequence of the Six-Day War of 1967. Israel's boundaries are the subject matter for Zechariah's second vision, specifically contended by the Jews and the Palestinians. The wider and collective Arab nations are also involved, which will result in war, arguably, around the commencement of the tribulation (Ps. 83), and Russia will also be at war with Israel during the latter part of the tribulation (Ezek. 38-39, Dan. 11:40-45).

Again, the dispute between the Jews and the Palestinians and Arabs centers on who owns the land. The four-thousand-year-old Arab-Israel conflict is no small problem as it will result in the next major war (Ps. 83, Isa. 17) and world war (Ezek. 38-39, Dan. 11:40-45, Rev. 16:14-16). The coming war described by Asaph (Ps. 83) and Isaiah (chapter 17) will probably occur at the beginning of the tribulation, catalysing the establishment of the (false) prophesied peace treaty (Isa. 28:14-16, 18), thereby triggering the (seven-year) hour of trial (Rev. 3:10, cf. Dan 9:24-27), ending with the battle of Armageddon (Dan. 11:40-45, Rev. 9:13-19, 16:14-16, Rev. 19:11-21).

Despite all the noise about who owns what, God makes it abundantly clear that He owns and holds the land (Zech. 1:14, 17, 2:13) and all else for that matter (Ps. 24:1). As for those claiming the land for themselves, the Bible is not silent, "For behold, your enemies make an uproar; those who hate you have raised their heads. They lay crafty plans against your people; they consult together against your treasured ones. They say, "Come, let us wipe them out as a nation; let the name of Israel be remembered no more!" (Ps 83:4-5), and who say, "Let us take possession for ourselves of the pastures of God" (Ps. 83:11). The psalmist, Asaph responds, "O my God, make them like whirling dust, like chaff before the wind. As fire consumes the forest, as the flame sets the mountains ablaze, so may You pursue them with Your tempest and terrify them with Your hurricane! Fill their faces with shame, that they may seek Your name, O Lord. Let them be put to shame and dismayed forever; let them perish in disgrace, that they may know that You alone, whose name is the Lord, are the Most High over all the earth" (Ps. 83:13-18). In sum, the psalmist states that Jerusalem belongs to God and the people of God. Zechariah, verses four, five, and twelve could not be more precise on the matter. God will personally respond to the nations claiming the land; He will choose and protect the city and His people who dwell within (Zech. 2:5,10, 11, 12, 13).

Following God setting Israel's borders (Zech. 2:2), He warns the nations which He is exceedingly angry with (Zech. 1:15) that Israel is the apple of His eye. - this means the 'most vulnerable part in need of the most protection.' Anyone touching the city of Jerusalem, where His people dwell, touches the most sensitive part of God's being. Thus, He will respond accordingly (Zech. 2:9. cf. Hag. 2:6, 21). God will shake the very nations He sent to plunder Israel (Zech. 2:8). As mentioned in the previous section, God sends the nations to produce salvation in His people (Zech. chapters 10, 12 & 13) during the tribulation and then judges the nations after the time of trouble (Matt. 25:41-46). So severe will be the judgement on the nations that God will silence all flesh who seek to harm His people and quarrel over the land (Zech. 2:13). Simply put, He will put a permanent end to them and or their claims.

Like in the days of Zechariah, leading into the tribulation, in preparation for the things to come, God makes the last call. He urgently calls every Jew living outside of the walls of Jerusalem, who have been scattered throughout the world (Zech. 2:6), to return, quickly, "Up! up! Flee" (Zech. 2:6), "Up, escape to Zion" (Zech. 2:7). The scattering refers to the literal spreading from the Babylonians, then speaking to those who still have not returned to Jerusalem and prophetically still speaks to the Jews in these last days. The last scattering occurred in 70 A.D, leaving the Jews without a homeland until 1948. The Jews are now being called back to Israel in preparation for the tribulation and salvation (Zech. 10:8, cf. Rom 11:25-32). Therefore, and again, the passage has double references, such as the prophecies of Isaiah, being fulfilled in two parts (Isa. 9:6-7, 61:1-2).

The term for Jews returning to Israel is Aliyah, meaning 'Going up'. The original expression regarded worship and was used by a Jew 'Going up' to read scripture (the Torah) publicly. The prophecy of the Jews returning home commenced its fulfilment when Israel was rebirthed (Ezek. 37:1-14, cf. Matt. 24:32-35). When Israel became a nation, again, on a signal day (Isa. 66:7-9), then the Jews were then summoned to return for the purpose of knowing God (Ezek. 37:12-14). They have been returning from every nation where God scattered them since Israel's reformation (Zech. 2:6, cf. Ezek. 11:17) for over seventy years now, yet not without conflict. The conflict will even escalate (Matt. 24:9-28) until Jesus returns at the end of the tribulation (Matt. 24:29-31).

So far, and in sum, from the above-mentioned, Zechariah's vision communicates three proclamations, 1). The land of Israel belongs to God; 2). After Jesus has dealt with the nations, He will reclaim and dwell in the holy land; and 3). When Jesus is ruling and reigning on the earth from the holy land, the nations will be silenced, and all will worship Him (Zech. 2:11, 13, 14:16-21). At that time, when Jesus returns to the earth, His glory will fill the temple (Ezek. 24:2-5). Not just the temple but the city of Jerusalem (Zech. 2:5, 11), the whole land (Zech. 2:12, 14:20-21), and the entire world (Hab. 2:14). However, and as mentioned earlier, before Jesus sets up His millennial kingdom, He will judge the nations throughout the tribulation. Just before judging the nations, Jesus will gather His people out of, "Babylon" (Zech. 2:7) and "into His midst" (Zech. 2:5, 10, 11, 13).

Interestingly, while God seeks to dwell with His people (Zech. 2:5, 9, 10, 13), His people are comfortably dwelling in Babylon (Zech. 2:7). The call to, "Come out" of Babylon mirrors Revelation, chapter eighteen (v. 4), where God is about to judge the Babylonian world system, paying her back, as she has paid others (Zech. 2:8-9, 13, Rev.18:6), in fact, double for the trouble (Rev. 18:6b). The same message is given to the church of Laodicea (Rev. 3:15-18). The warning to all is that God will judge Babylon (the world system and worldly religion) at the end of the tribulation. In a single day (Rev. 18:8), in a single hour (Rev. 18:10b, 17, 19), she will be no more, no more, no more, no more, no more, no more (x6 Rev. 18:21-23). Anyone clinging to Babylon will share in her punishment (Rev. 18:4, cf. Rom 1:32). By judging the world, God will reveal Himself to all people (Zech. 2:10) who, all-accepting, will know that He is their God and their deliverer (Zech. 2:9, 11).

Again, the judgement of the nations will take place just before entering the millennial reign, where there will be an extended invitation to all (whoever is left) to enter God's rest (Zech. 12:10, 13:1, 14:16). On the grounds of the above-mentioned, the passage confirms that the promise is not yet fulfilled and is not just extended to Israel, but all nations, that they too may enter God's dwelling place and be His people (Zech. 2:11).

To reiterate, following the judgment, not just the Jews will know and fear Jesus in the holy land throughout the millennium, but people from every nation will come to know and worship Him (cf. Zech. 2:11, 8:20–23; 14:16-21; Isa. 2:3). While the term 'Holy land' is commonly known as the biblical phrase for Israel; it is only found in Zechariah's book (Zech. 2:12) and the Psalms (Ps. 78:54). This refers to the Lord's inheritance (cf. Zech. 8:3), and Jerusalem as His choice (cf. Zech. 1:17; 2;12, 3:2) to be the capital of the world (Isa. 2:1–2).

In conclusion, "On that day" (Zech. 3:10, 9:16, 11:11, 12:3, 4, 6, 8, 9, 11, 13:1, 2, 4, 14:4, 6, 8, 9, 13, 20, 21) following Jesus' wrath being poured out (Rev. 6:16-17) and completed (Rev. 15:1, 16:17), He will return. Many nations will join themselves to Him (Zech. 2:11) alongside Israel (Zech. 2:12). Those who do will inherit the kingdom because they have Christ. In fact, because of Israel the nations submit to God (Rev. 7), thereby sharing in their millennial inheritance. When Jesus returns, God will inherit Judah in the holy land choosing Jerusalem (Zech. 1:17, 2:12, Hab. 2:20) for Himself, once more, from where He will rule and reign, and the saints will co-rule with Him for one thousand years (Rev. 5:10, 11:15, 20:2-7).

In the meantime, the words, "Run" (Zech. 2:4), "Up, up! Flee" (Zech. 2:6), and "Up! Escape" (Zech. 2:7) are purposed to motivate the hearer, giving the reader a sense of urgency now, as they did then. "In a little while" (Hag. 2:6), what is about to happen, will happen quickly! Such was the case for the part fulfilling of this prophecy in Zechariah's time and will be the case for the fulfilment in our own (cf. 1 Thess. 5:3).

Today, those exact words are now being echoed loudly. Run. Up, up! Flee. Up! Escape (Rev. 18) for those with an ear to hear. God is about to pour out His wrath, resulting in great tribulation for this world, such has never been seen before or will be again (Jer. 30:7, Dan. 12:1, Matt. 24:21). The call to flee and escape is first and foremost to the individual (Zech. 2:4-5), then to the nation Israel and the church (Zech. 2:6-12, cf. Rev. 2-3), followed by the world (Zech. 2:13). All must flee to escape the things to come.

In sum, the proclamation of Zechariah chapter two is that Jesus is returning to the earth, coming to judge the nations, reclaim Israel, and set up His millennial kingdom, where He will dwell with His people (Zech. 2:5, 10, 11, 13, 3:14-15). On that day, the entire human race will bow in silence and awe before the Almighty God (Zech. 2:13). The prophet Haggai saw and confirmed the same, "The LORD is in His holy temple; let all the earth keep silence before Him" (Hag. 2:20). When Jesus returns, He will put an end to the debate, about who owns the land. He does!

CHAPTER THREE

JOSHUA THE HIGH PRIEST

'Plucked from the Fire'
(Zech. 3:1-10)

In previous visions and chapters, God focuses on external issues, that is, what is outside the wall. Now He narrows in on matters closer to home, the heart, or more to the point, the condition of the heart.

Directly linked with the opening verse (Zech. 3:1) is another, found in the book of Revelation (Rev. 12:10), where John's vision and revelation reveal Satan, the accuser of the brethren, is hard at work. In Zechariah's vision, Satan accuses Joshua of being a sinner (Zech. 3:3), and the accusation is correct! Joshua is a sinner; he is dressed in filthy rags (Zech. 3:4). However, Joshua (Zech. 3:1, 3, 6, 8, 9, 6:11) is also the high priest (Zech. 3:1, 8, 6:11), representing Israel (Zech. 3:2) and is a sign for Israel (Zech. 3:8), presenting future salvation where God will in a single day (Zech. 3:9), remove their sin (Zech. 3:4, 9).

Note the sitting of the passage; it is a court of law. Joshua is standing before the Judge (God), guilty, due to wearing filthy rob. However, his filthy rob is exchanged for a clean one, and he is also given a (white) stone, and allowed to sit. While all the while, his accuser (Satan) in condemning him. However, the Lord rebukes the accuser (Satan) (Zech. 3:2), and Michael, the archangel, voiced the same when contesting Satan over Moses' body (Jude 1:9). Over what God has chosen, Satan has no claim. In other words, you cannot curse what God has blessed (Num. 23:8). In the case of Zechariah's vision, God had chosen Jerusalem (Zech. 2:12, 3:2) and the people who are to inherit the city during the millennium as a, "Brand plucked out of the fire" (Zech. 3:2).

God fulfilled His part of that covenant promise some two thousand years ago through the death and resurrection of Jesus. However, due to Israel's failure to accept Christ as their Messiah, the Jews did not and will not experience the benefits of the finished work until after the tribulation. The benefit, namely, is salvation through Jesus Christ alone (Jn. 14:6, Acts 4:12), through faith (in Christ) alone (Esp. 2:8-9), we are saved.

During the time of trouble, the Jews will, once again, be given an opportunity to come to a saving knowledge (Rev. 7:14, 19:8) of the One they crucified (Zech. 12:10b-11), in order to be saved (cf. Zech. 3:2, 4-5, 13:1). But first, they will have to call on His name (Zech. 12:10a, Rom. 10:8-13), sealing them by the Holy Spirit. Once sealed, the Jews will usher in the return of the Messiah (Matt. 23:39). After the Gentiles have been removed (Rom. 11:25, 2 Thess. 2:7, Rev. 3:10, 4:1), the Jews will then be reinstated (Zech. 3:4a, Rom. 11:25-32), but not before. Then, those confessing Christ will exchange their filthy rags for pure garments (Zech. 3:4b, cf. Isa. 64:6). On that day (Zech. 3:10), during the tribulation, the Jews will 'then' be able to meet the covenant requirements, appeasing God's wrath (Isa. 64:9, 12). Like all covenant promises, their inheritance is conditional on them doing their part (Zech. 3:6). "IF you walk in My ways...,"

On that day, by meeting the conditional "IF," Joshua (Israel, the Jews) will receive three millennial blessings, 1). They will rule God's house; 2).

They will have charge over God's courts, and 3). They will have the right to access (Zech. 3:7).

Notice the comparison between verses one and four, and in verse eight, Joshua is first seen standing before the angel of the Lord (Zech. 3:1, 4), and then later (Zech. 3:8), he is seated. Verse one represents judgment through examination (Zech. 1:9), and verse eight describes the finished work. Having undergone the judgment and being found innocent, therefore acquitted, a stone is set before Joshua (Zech. 3:9).

The 'Stone' (Zech. 3:9) is symbolic of innocence (Rev. 2:17) and is given to the one who conquers and remains conquering by putting their faith in Jesus, alone. Besides trusting in Jesus, repentance is the key to salvation and keeping it (cf. Zech. 1:3), which is continual obedience (Zech. 3:7). The one who is given the white stone is, only because they have the Stone, Jesus.

Repentance and faithfulness go hand in hand, which brings us back to the conditional "If" (Zech. 3:6). Contrary to what some suggest, repentance has nothing to do with worked-based salvation but is the evidence of salvation, bearing first (Matt. 3:8). Repentance is also the evidence of the Holy Spirit working within, which is likewise the evidence of salvation. The one who has the Spirit has Christ (1 Jn. 3:24, 4:13), who is the Servant, Branch, and the Stone.

The reference to the 'Servant' (Zech. 3:8, cf. Isa. 53:11), the 'Branch' (Zech. 3:8, 6:12-13), and the 'Stone' (Zech. 3:9, Matt. 21:42) are all Messianic symbolism, pointing to Jesus, the Saviour - the One, the One and Only One who can save (Jn. 14:6, Acts 4:12). The very 'Stone' (Zech. 3:9) (Jesus) that Israel stumbled over (Rom. 9:31-33) will at a future date be set before them, once more, yet only after He (Jesus) is acknowledged and accepted by Israel. Then, He will be given to them. And then, He will take away their sin (Zech. 3:4, 9).

However, before then, the Rock (Jesus) they rejected will first crush them during the tribulation. "Therefore, I tell you that the kingdom of God will be taken away from you and given to a people who will produce its fruit. He who falls on this Stone will be broken to pieces, but he on whom it falls will be crushed." (Matt. 21:43-44). During the tribulation, the Jews will be crushed through persecution, releasing a sweet aroma of faithfulness unto God, just like the church of Smyrna (Rev. 2:8-11). Like Smyrna, the Jews will be, "Tested for ten (many) days" (Rev. 2:10).

Being tested refers to undergoing a 'close examination'. Keeping verses one and four (standing) and eight (seated) in mind (Zech. 3:1, 4, 8), Zechariah narrows in on the examination using the reference of "Seven eyes" (Zech. 3:9). The seven eyes on the stone symbolise the Holy Spirit (Isa. 11:2; Rev. 5:6). In the following chapter, Zechariah picks up on the same again, "These seven are the eyes of the Lord, which range through the whole earth" (Zech. 4:10). Both references (Zech. 3:9, 4:10) symbolise God's worldwide scrutiny, where nothing is hidden, everything is thoroughly examined and fully exposed. The examination's first and last area determined whether or not the one being tested has the Stone, Jesus Christ? If the answer is yes, the Judge finds the defendant innocent (Zech. 3:4-5), they are acquitted, and the trial is over. If not, the defendant will be found guilty and then sentenced according to their works (cf. Rev. 19:11-15). The greatest sin anyone can commit is to reject, or not have, Jesus Christ, and therefore lack His Spirit who reveals Him (cf. Matt. 16:17).

While the Jews were first invited to enter the promise of salvation, they still have not due to failing to meet the conditional requirement. However, they will, and as promised, they will be grafted back in (Rom. 11:24) after the fullness of the Gentiles (church) has come in (Rom. 11:25). Then, the promise to Israel will be fulfilled in a single day (Zech. 3:9, cf. Isa. 66:8), taking place after the tribulation (Zech. 13:1).

The term 'Single-day' (Zech. 3:9) refers to the combined judgement of the world followed by those trusting in Jesus (Rev. 18:8). The judgement will occur in a single hour (Rev. 18:10, 17, 19). Albeit, amidst great tribulation, salvation is always on offer (Rev. 18:4). Note, the salvation promise is not just for Israel, but for Israel's 'friends' who sit before them (Zech. 3:8). The friends include people from the nations who joined themselves to the Jews during the tribulation; they also shall belong to the Lord (Zech. 2:11).

The friends of Israel are distinct from Israel's standing (Zech. 3:4, 7). These friends are seated, indicating they are priestly themselves. As a sign, they are presenting something futuristic also. The friends may include those who have gone before Israel in the rapture (Rev. 4:1 -the church. The church is seated before them, with Jesus, having entered Christ's finished work before the tribulation, raised and seated with Him (Eph. 2:6). However, again, the immediate context suggests the friends of Israel are joined with them in the tribulation (Zech. 2:11). John provides more information in chapter twelve of the book of Revelation, referring to Israel's "Offspring" (Rev. 12:17). Israel's offspring are those who have come to faith in Jesus through the testimony of the sealed Jewish evangelists (Zech. 8:22, Rev. 7). The offspring will be a 'Great multitude', representative of every nation (Rev. 7:9). Many of those who come to faith through the Jews will die in the tribulation (Rev. 7:14).

Following the tribulation, "On that Day" (Zech. 3:10), the resurrected tribulation saints (Rev. 19:6) will then share in the inheritance of the threefold covenantal promise (Zech. 3:6). Following Israel, the saints will rule and reign with Jesus, having unrestricted access to Him (Zech. 2:11).

The ministry of the redeemed Jews will fulfil what Jesus said must happen before He returns, "This gospel of the kingdom will be proclaimed throughout the whole world as a testimony to all nations, and then the end will come" (Matt. 24:14). The Jews will be the ones who proclaim the gospel throughout the tribulation (Rev. 7, 11, 14:1-5). Indeed, both now and then, salvation is from the Jews (Jn. 4:22, Acts 13:23, Rom. 3:2).

In sum, the direct application of the chapter (Zech. 3) is that Israel will come to a revelation and a saving knowledge of Jesus Christ during the tribulation period. This will last seven years, where they will then be "Plucked from the fire" (Zech. 3:2). Israel has been plucked from the fire before (Amos. 4:11); however, they did not return or remain obedient. In other words, they failed to keep the covenant requirement, "If you walk in My ways and keep the charge" (Zech. 3:7). During the time of testing, God will return to them if they return to Him (Zech. 1:3). God will also include the nations in Israel's extended grace (Zech. 2:11, 8:22, cf. 12:10). During that same time, Satan will go after the Jews like never before (Rev. 12), using the nations that God sends to scatter them (Zech. 1:21). The events that unfold during the seven years cannot be compared to anything in history, nor anything again after the tribulation (Matt. 24:21-26).

The direct application applies to the Jews who will not escape the hour of trial coming upon the whole world (Rev. 3:10). The trial is also known as the wrath of the Lamb (Rev. 6:16) and the wrath of God (Rev. 14:19, 16:1), which is the same wrath the church is destined to escape (1 Thess. 1:10, 5:9). However, alongside the Jews, the majority within the church ('confessing' Christians) will likewise be left behind (Matt. 7:21-23). This is due to not meeting the mixed requirement of belief and obedience (2 Thess. 1:8), thereby failing to qualify for having "Their iniquity taken away." Those failing the test do so due to failing, "Walk in God's ways and keep His charge" (Zech. 1:7). A New Testament equivalent would be to, "Keep themselves in the love of God" (Jude 1:21) therefore, be, or remain to be, "Snatched out of the fire" (Jude 1:23a, cf. Amos 4:11).

The term 'Snatched out of the fire' refers to sin, confirmed by Jude's following statement, "Hating the garment stained by the flesh" (Jude. 1:23b).

Those who do come to Christ and keep themselves within the love of God will not only escape the things to come, but they will rule and reign with Christ during the millennium (Rev. 1:6, 2:25-27, 5:10, 11:15, cf. Zech. 3:7). Remaining within the covenant is the requirement ("If you walk in My ways" Zech. 3:7), remembering, Israel had once been, "Plucked out of the fire" (Amos 4:11a) before, and they. "Did not return" (Amos 4:11b). Therefore the pronouncement was, "Prepare to meet your God!" (Amos 4:11).

During the tribulation, Israel will indeed 'Meet their God' while the saints are safe and secure in heaven (Rev. 4:1), where Satan, their accuser (Rev. 12:10), can no longer reach them. Although the accuser will still curse the secured saints from the ground, "It (the antichrist) opened its mouth to utter blasphemies against God, blaspheming His name and His dwelling, that is, those who dwell in heaven" (Rev. 13:6). Satan blasphemes God through his son of perdition, the antichrist. Satan, however, can curse the saints all he likes, for the response from heaven will be, "The Lord rebukes you O Satan, Is this not a brand plucked from the fire?" (Zech. 3:2).

In conclusion, the offer to all here and now is to be plucked from the fire, this side of the tribulation, or at least, during the tribulation, otherwise, perish eternally.

CHAPTER FOUR

THE TWO LAMPSTANDS

'Not by Might, Nor by Power'
(Zech. 4:1-14)

Following the previous chapters, with one continuous vision, segmented into eight parts, Zechariah was woken by the angel suddenly (Zech. 4:1). The angel asked, "What do you see?" (Zech. 4:2, 5:2). Until now, the prophet asked the angel, "What are these?" (Zech. 1:9, 19, 21). This time, it is the other way around, and Zechariah answers the question by saying that he sees a "Lampstand" with "Seven tips and lamps on top" (Zech. 4:2). The prophet also sees "Two olive trees" (Zech. 4:3).

The lampstands were of particular interest. While familiar to any practicing Jew, Zechariah had difficulty understanding what he was shown; such was the case with the other visions (cf. Zech. 1:9, 19; 4:11; 6:4; cf. 5:6). Therefore, the prophet asked the question five times more, "What are these?" (Zech. 4:4, 5, 11, 12, 13). Again, Zechariah's inquiries referred to the lamps and olive trees; the latter is finally answered in verse fourteen, "These are the two anointed ones who stand by the Lord of the whole earth."

Before addressing the two olive trees (Zech. 4:3), being the two anointed ones (Zech. 4:14), the angel thought it was necessary to first focus on the topic of the temple (Zech. 4:9). Remember, the topic of the temple has been an ongoing theme as introduced by Ezra (4:24-5:1-2) and Haggai (1:1-11-2:1-9). Now, in this fifth vision, the angel introduces the topic of the temple to Zechariah, also wanting to clarify that it will be built by God, not man; not by man's strength or through his power and ability, but God's alone (Zech. 4:6).

The angel also wants to make the point that the idea or desire to rebuild the temple is not motivated by man; in the same way, the project will not be managed by man, no matter how capable, resourceful, or powerful he thinks he thinks is. The evidence is seen through the book of Haggai, where the Jews had neglected the temple rebuild in pursuit of lining their own pockets (Hag. 1:2-6). For doing this, God rebuked Judah (Hag. 1:7), instructing them to return and rebuild or else! (Hag. 1:7-11). Seen through the prophets Haggai and Zechariah, God rebuilds the temple through the hands of men (Zech. 4:9, 6:15).

Through verse seven, further support and confirmation for God rebuilding the temple, not man, is seen (Zech. 4:7). Despite the numerous challenges that stand in the way of the project, every "Mighty Mountain" (Zech. 4:7) or challenge and obstacle would be removed, supernaturally, pointing out even more that God is managing this heavenly project. So evident will it be that every critic will be silenced, even turning their negativity into rejoicing (Zech. 4:10). The critics being silenced is a repeat of chapter two, where God will, "Silence all flesh" (Zech. 2:13) regarding Israel's boundaries (Zech. 2:1-2) that the nations currently squabble over (Zech. 1:15).

Now that the angel has made it clear, God will build His house (Zech. 4:6, cf. Matt. 16:18), in this case being the temple, the following point is that He will rebuild it, or at least commence the rebuild, before the two anointed ones (Zech. 4:3, 14) appear and can be identified. The reason is that their ministry is connected, and will coincide with the rebuilt temple, that is the third temple, not the second (cf. Rev. 11). Zechariah, chapter four, verse fourteen, confirms the fulfilled timing of the prophecy with the two anointed ones standing by the Lord of the whole earth (Zech. 4:14, Rev. 11:4). As with the previous chapters, the visions jump two thousand, five hundred years from the current day, to our own. The two olive trees are the two witnesses (Zech. 4:3, 14, Rev. 11:4).

Further confirmation of the future fulfilment is seen through how God measured out Israel's boundaries after the tribulation (Zech. 2:1-2). During the tribulation, He measures the third temple and alter. This event occurs around the midpoint of the coming seven-year ordeal (Rev. 11:1, 2, 3). After the third temple is rebuilt, the outside courts are not measured due to the nations trampling it for forty-two months (Rev. 11:2), concluding the tribulation. Jesus concurred; that the Gentiles will trample Jerusalem until He returns (Lu. 21:24).

Before addressing the two anointed ones, or witnesses, the significance of the temple is that it is a place of worship, where God is known and made known. Today, from the temple, literal or symbolic of the Body of Christ (1 Cor. 3:16, 6:19), the gospel is and was always purposed to go out into the world. In the book of Revelation, there is a reference to seven lampstands, which are symbolic of the churches (Rev. 1:20). The Holy Spirit represents the oil, or anointing (Zech. 4:6). After the church has been removed, the lampstands Zechariah saw will fulfil the Jewish mandate, as representatives of both God and Israel and as a light to the nations (cf. Isa. 42:6; 49:6) during the tribulation.

The phrase, "Grace, grace to it" (Zech. 4:7b) relates to God's might and power, removing every obstacle standing in the way of the temple rebuild, giving every opportunity to obey and serve God. For Zechariah's audience, God's grace enabled them to build the second temple. During the tribulation, the grace of God will be extended to all, calling them, and empowering survivors to repent through the enabling Spirit of grace (Zech. 12:10, Heb. 10:29). During the tribulation, and after it, the Spirit will, "Range through the whole earth" (Zech. 4:10) examining every person; rewarding them, for good or for bad, according to what they did with the invitation of salvation (cf. Matt. 16:27, Rev. 2:23, 20:12).

During the tribulation, there is an extending time of grace, administered through the two witnesses (candlesticks), who preach the gospel from outside of the temple walls, as the temple itself will be defiled (Dan. 12:11, Matt. 24:15, 2 Thess. 2:4). Those worshipping within are also defiled and accounted for (Rev. 11:1b). Although the temple is defiled, God still authorises it (Rev. 11:1a) in the same way He gives the antichrist dominion (Dan. 7:6, 26) for seven years (Dan. 12:7). During the tribulation, the third temple will be the beast's seat (2 Thess. 2:4), meaning, from where he rules, albeit, not without opposition. The message of the antichrist, the false prophet, and that of the two witnesses promote two different messiahs, in the same way false prophets and preachers do today (2 Cor. 11:4). Two false witnesses will promote a false messiah (the antichrist) - while two true witnesses will proclaim the Messiah (Jesus Christ).

Given that Zechariah's prophecy is to Judah and will be fulfilled in the tribulation, the nationality of the two witnesses is Jewish (cf. Rev. 11:3). Being "Olive trees" (Zech. 4:3, 11, Rev. 11:4) they are anointed as priestly prophets who will preach the gospel to the world, from the temple courts, fulfilling the Olivet discord prophecy, (Matt 24:14). Through the two witnesses, alongside the 144,000 Jewish evangelists (Rev. 7, 14:1-5) "The gospel will be proclaimed throughout the whole world." Nothing more is said of the two witnesses through Zechariah or anywhere else other than what is found in the book of Revelation (Rev. 11).

In sum, from the book of Revelation, Zechariah's two anointed ones (Zech. 4:3, 14), or witnesses (Rev. 11:4) are seen preaching the gospel of the kingdom to the whole world during the second half of the tribulation period (Rev. 11:3–6, esp. v. 3). They will appear when the third temple is rebuilt (Zech. 4:6-10, Rev. 11:2-3), from where the antichrist announces he is God at the halfway point of the seven-year ordeal (Matt 24:15, Dan. 9:27, 11:31, 12:11).

These witnesses are dressed in sackcloth, which again is a Jewish custom, confirming they are Jewish, representing repentance. Therefore, their gospel message will be one of repentance, pointing to Christ, which is why the world will hate them so and be tormented by their message (Rev. 11:10, cf. 9:20-21, 16:8-11). Adding to the torment, these two lampstands will operate in unstoppable power through signs and wonders (Rev. 11:5-6) due to being anointed by God (Zech. 4:14). They will preach for three-and-a-half years (Rev. 11:2, 3), removing every mountain of resistance (Zech. 4:7), which is the same timeframe Jesus preached. Then, after their ministry is complete, the antichrist will kill them (Rev. 11:7-8). Once killed, the world will rejoice over their deaths and will even exchange gifts (Rev. 11:9, 10). However, as Christ did, the two witnesses will rise again three days later (Rev. 11:11), even from the same place Jesus was crucified (Rev. 11:8). Then, "Great fear" will come over all that see them risen from the grave (Rev. 11:11) and raptured into heaven (Rev. 11:12). Then the rest surviving the following earthquake will be terrified (Rev. 11:13), which will be absolutely everyone, due to live internet streaming.

Interestingly, the two witnesses' resurrection follows the antichrist's resurrection, which probably occurred three and a half years earlier due to receiving a mortal wound (Rev. 12:3, 12, 14). In the tribulation, the antichrist will be killed and will descend into the bottomless pit (Rev. 11:7, 17:8). The beast (antichrist), "Who was, and was not, rises again" (Rev. 17:8 [twice], 11). Satan resurrects the antichrist, giving him his power (2 Thess. 2:9), but God sends him (2 Thess. 2:11); therefore, God remains sovereign overall. Note the wording regarding the resurrection of the antichrist, "Who was and was not, and rises," counterfeiting Jesus Christ (Rev. 1:4, 8, 4:8). The resurrection of the antichrist will be a great deceiving sign (Rev. 13:13, cf. Matt. 24:24, 2 Thess. 2:9-11), occurring somewhere around the tribulation midpoint, causing the whole world to marvel (Rev. 13:3, 17:8). Once the antichrist spellbinds the world, he will announce that he is God (Dan. 7:8, 20, Matt. 24:15, 2 Thess. 2:9-11). Later, he will kill the two witnesses once their ministry is finished (Rev. 11:7). Once more, God is sovereign.

After a short time of being resurrected, the witnesses will then be raptured (Rev. 11:12). The words, "Come up here" repeat Revelation, chapter four (Rev. 4:1), which is symbolic of the church being raptured just before the tribulation commences. When the church hears those words, "Come up here" Christ meets them in the air (1 Thess. 4:17). The same is true for the two witnesses at the end of the tribulation, where Christ is on route to earth, with ten thousand saints following (Jude 1:4). Remember, the church does not go through the tribulation (1 Thess. 1:10, 5:9, 2 Thess. 6-8, Rev. 3:10, 4:1). As with the rapture of the church, the whole world will witness the ascent of the two witnesses into heaven (Rev. 11:12), which contributes to the cause of great fear (Rev. 11:13).

As for the identity of the two witnesses, like with the unknown identity of the antichrist and the false prophet, the identity of the two witnesses is not fully known. However, an argument could be made that one is Elijah, revealed through the prophet Malachi (Mal. 4:5-6). The other witness is suspected to be Moses. Moses is most likely to join Elijah due to the similarity of the plagues on Egypt with the tribulation plagues, the Law being preached in the tribulation (Rev. 12:17, 14:12), and accompanying Elijah at the Mount of Transfiguration (Matt. 17). Moses is also referenced in Revelation, chapter fifteen (Rev. 15:3), suggesting that he is present during the ordeal. However, some claim that instead of Moses, Enoch is the other witness due to not seeing death (cf. Heb. 9:27) and his apocalyptic contribution through the book of Enoch, albeit apocryphal. Others again suggest Gad and Nathan are the two witnesses.

    The argument made for the prophets Gad and Nathan to fulfil the prophecy is loosely drawn from First Chronicles (1 Chron. 29:29). The apparent connection for Gad is sketched in First Chronicles, chapter twenty-one (1 Chron. 21:11-12), where the prophet gives David a choice of one of three judgements to choose from. The link (or leap) to Revelation, chapter eleven is made where similar judgements are administered through the two witnesses (Rev. 11:5-6). For example, drought is a plague distributed through the two witnesses (Rev. 11:6) as one of the choices given to David (1 Chron. 21:12). Like Nathan (2 Sam. 12:1-14), Gad confronts David and predicts judgement through famine to fall upon the kingdom. A lack of rain results in famine (cf. Zech. 14:18). The connection is a stretch, at best. Another exaggerated link to the Revelation witnesses and Gad, the seer, is turning water into blood (Rev. 11:6, 1 Chron. 21:12). The association draws a longbow where subscribers state due to the amount of bloodshed over three months the waters would be blood-soaked, therefore, turned to blood. Yet another correlation is claimed through the ability to cause pestilence (Rev. 11:6, 1 Chron. 21:12). However, Gad was only the messenger, not the facilitator; therefore, the view is flawed.

    As seen above, the identity of the two witnesses varies. Yet, regardless of who they are, one thing is known, they are Jewish prophets, and they will be present and revealed in the second part of the tribulation (Rev.

11:3), after the temple has been completed (Rev. 11:1). The witnesses will appear when Satan is cast to the earth (Rev. 11:14, 12:9), which is a sub-woe (Rev. 12:12) of the seven-year ordeal. During the tribulation, there are three, "Woes" (Rev. 8:13), concurring with the following three trumpets (5th, 6th, and 7th) judgements. Satan is cast to the earth between the first and second woe (5th and 6th trumpet), confirmed by Revelation, chapter eleven (v. 14). The second woe (Rev. 8:13) refers to the 200m mounted troops (Rev. 913-19) who invade Jerusalem (Rev. 16:14-16, cf. Dan. 11:40-45) towards the end of the tribulation. When the troops enter Jerusalem, they, "Trample" the holy city (Rev. 11:2, Lu. 21:24).

From the time Satan is cast to the earth, the Jews suffer the greatest persecution ever experienced, directly from the devil (Rev. 12:15), through the antichrist (Dan. 7, 9, 11, 12), causing them to flee for forty-two months (Rev. 12:6, 14, Isa. 26:20-21, Matt. 24:16). After forty-two months, the last trumpet is blown (3rd woe), resulting in the return of Jesus Christ (Rev. 11:15-19, 19:11-21). The return of Jesus Christ is the third woe of the tribulation for those not ready or refusing to fear and worship Him (Rev. 14:7). The two witnesses will point to Christ, preaching the gospel for forty-two months, empowered by God, warning of the coming judgement (Rev. 11:3). Angels will also join in (Rev. 14:6-13), backing up the 144,000 Jewish evangelists (Rev. 7. 14:1-4). The message from all will be, Repent, and, "Return to Me, and (then) I will return to you" (Zech. 1:3). The message never changes, as seen through the letters to the seven churches (Rev. 2-3).

*Important note: Until now, I have said that the two witnesses appear at the beginning of the tribulation and will perish halfway through. However, I have changed my position for the reasons that are mentioned above.

In conclusion, both within the time of Zechariah and during the tribulation, God did and will accomplish what He said He would do through

His power and by His Spirit. In fact, His word is as good as done, from beginning to end (Rev. 21:5, 22:6, Ps. 119:89, Isa. 55:11). During the tribulation, God will extend a time of grace through His Spirit of grace (Zech. 12:10), revealing Himself through the anointed Jewish witnesses, among others, giving every person an opportunity to repent and or return (cf. Ezek. 18:32, 2 Pet. 3:9). After the tribulation, God will judge the Jews and the nations, settling every matter (Zech. 2:13, cf. Ps. 145).

The Holy Spirit will examine and testify as to what was done with the gospel of Jesus Christ (Isa. 11:2, Zech. 4:10, Rev. 3:1). Jesus, who was preached throughout the time of trouble, will return to set up His millennial kingdom which will include removing the defiled tribulation temple and replacing it with the heavenly temple brought down to earth. During the millennium, the temple will remain aloft (Zech. 14:10), preventing the millennial's access. More on that in chapter fourteen.

CHAPTER FIVE

FLYING SCROLL

'The Woman in the Basket'
(Zech. 5:1-11)

As with the previous visions (one to five), the theme of chapter five is judgement, introduced through the flying scroll. Likewise, the appointed time for the judgement is the tribulation. Again, Israel is the focus due to the continuous religious sin of the Jews. For their sin, they and the whole land are under a curse (Zech. 5:3). As mentioned in chapter one, the curse's origin is found in Deuteronomy, chapters twenty-eight and thirty (blessings and curses). Judah's ancestors were the original inheritors of the curse (Zech. 1:1-6), followed by the Jews of Jesus' day (Matt. 24:2, Mk. 13:2, Lu. 21:6, fulfilled in 70 A.D). The generation of Jews today, from those who witnessed Israel's rebirth (Matt. 24:32-35), will again find themselves coming head-to-head with the same curse, worse than ever before (Jer. 30:7, Dan. 12:1, Matt. 24:21). In fact, they have been under it since they rejected Jesus (Matt. 23:37-39) and again rejected the apostle Paul (Acts 18:5-6). Due to their rejection of the truth, they have been spiritually blinded (Zep. 1:17, Matt. 15:14, Jn. 9:37, 12:14, Rom.

11:25), as have many within the lukewarm, prosperity-driven church (Rev. 3:17).

The flying scroll of chapter five gives the reason for the curse, having two sides, significant to the Law (Ex. 32:15), which is broken. The scroll pronounces the curse (v. 3) due to breaching the third and eighth commandments, swearing falsely, and stealing (Ex. 20:7, 15, Zech. 5:3, 4), producing iniquity in the whole land (Zech. 5:6). On one side of the scroll, the announcement is: "Everyone who steals shall be cleaned out" (Zech. 5:4a), and on the other: "Everyone who swears falsely shall be cleaned out" (Zech. 5:4b).

Alongside the words, the measurement of the open scroll is also significant, like that of the temple (Zech. 2:1-3). This supports the idea that Israel's sin is spread throughout the land through their religious rituals and routines. Nothing has remained sacred; absolutely everything has been defiled. But as mentioned in previous sections, their defilement will only be dwarfed by the abomination to come from the tribulation temple (Matt. 24:15, 2 Thess. 2:4).

Alongside the scroll announcing judgement, the word worth noting, is 'Flying', symbolic of swiftly moving, and when it arrives, it will quickly deal with those who violate God's commands. However, verses three and four suggest that the final judgment is set for a future date, which is congruent with the previous chapters. When the judgement does take full effect, it will remain in place. As seen through verse four, the scroll not only enters the thief's house but remains in the house, keeping it clean, somewhat like a "Strongman" would (Matt. 12:29. Lu. 11:21). The fact that the house remains clean points toward the future millennial fulfilment of the prophecy due to Jesus (the Strongman) ruling with a rod of iron (Rev. 2:17, 12:5, 19:15).

The scroll's judgement and swiftness are likened to the 'Little scroll' John ate while receiving the revelation, again from an angel, of the things to come (Rev. 10:1-2). The bitter, sweet scroll that John ate refers to the return of Jesus Christ. The mystery of the scroll is revealed through the seventh trumpet, which is the third woe of the tribulation (Rev. 11:15-19, cf. 8:13). The return of Jesus will be both bitter and sweet (Rev. 10:9-10). Bitter for those rejecting or disobeying Christ, but sweet for those accepting, looking for, and living for Him. Isaiah references something similar, using a bitter/sweet idiom (Isa. 5:20). Isaiah's address aims at the religious who twist scripture by calling right wrong and wrong right. Isaiah targets Israel's religious leaders, who 'think' they are following God, just like many in the church do today, yet, "Swear falsely" (Zech. 5:3). When Jesus returns (Rev. 6:12-17, 14:14-20, 17:14, 19:11-21), the false, who swear falsely, the thieves (Zech. 5:4), the basket and woman within, will be removed from the earth (Zech. 5:9-11).

Again, the sin of swearing falsely and stealing is so great that God measures it out against the actual size of the temple being rebuilt (Zech. 2:1-2). He also symbolises it through the image of the basket (Zech. 5:5-6), the sin is widespread and commercial, referring to religious-racketeering. Essentially, Israel's leaders have, once again, turned God's house into the den of thieves (Jer. 7:11, Matt. 21:13).

We gain this understanding from the basket, representing the woman's livelihood, which in context connects commercialism to religious practice. The idea here is the religious rulers were not only cheating and misusing God's name, "Swearing falsely" (Zech. 5:3-4); they were merchandising the message and God's people. So much so that the woman in the basket was FULL of iniquity (Zech. 5:6). Being "Full of iniquity" is linked to the previous statement; the entire religious practice is corrupt, and therefore, the whole land is full of wickedness (Zech. 5:8) and is cursed (Zech. 5:3).

Although the land was full of iniquity (Zech. 5:6), which is wickedness (Zech. 5:8), wickedness was at least contained, to some degree, and for now to the lowest degree (Zech. 5:8). When the basket lid was lifted (Zech. 5:7), a woman was seen sitting in the basket, called, "Wickedness" (Zech. 5:7-8). The woman signifies every evil practice, specifically religious ones. At the time of Zechariah's vision, the 'Woman' (or deeds of) is to be confined while in the land of Israel and later transported to Shinar, or Babylon, where a 'House' will be built for her (Zech. 5:9-11). The Hebrew word for 'House' is also translated as 'Dwelling place' (i.e., God's dwelling place) and 'Temple'. Therefore, the house probably refers to the third tribulation temple. When Jesus returns, He cleans the House out (Zech. 5:4) in the same way He cleared out the money traders from the temple (Matt. 21:12-17). Within the vision, God, through the angel, reveals to the prophet that iniquity and wickedness must be removed from the land. God's angels will carry it away (Zech. 5:9-10) from Israel to Babylon, reserved for the time of the coming tribulation. The woman in the basket, transported to Shinar, is Jezebel. She is discussed later in this section.

As mentioned earlier, God removes everything false and unclean at the commencement of the millennial dispensation, made evident through verse eleven. Before then, God deals with these wicked religious racketeers, as seen where the vision fast-forwards some two thousand, five hundred years into the future, focusing on Shinar (Zech. 5:11). Shinar is in Babylon. Again, verses nine to eleven support verses three and four, suggesting the fulfilment of this vision will take place at a future date. Shinar (Zech. 5:11), or Babylon (Gen. 11:2, Rev. 17-18), is directly linked to the tribulation Babylonian system mentioned in the book of Revelation (17:3-5), where the sin of idolatry is returned to its original place in the last days, the seven-year time of trouble. Revelation, chapters seventeen and eighteen narrow in on the fulfilment of Zechariah's prophetic vision, setting the stage for the final judgment, when Jesus returns (Rev. 19:11-21).

Previously stated and revealed through the sixth (Zech. 5:1-4) and seventh (Zech. 5:5-11) visions given to the prophet Zechariah, God's judgement is looming against the wicked, even roaming the earth, impatiently, as we speak (Zech. 1:10, 6:7). The coming judgement will be measured out to all, including the Jews (Zech. 1:2, 4-5, 10:3, 11:1-17, 13:7-9) and the Gentiles (Zech. 1:15, 9:1-8, 14:1-5, 12-15). The angel clarifies that God's judgement is against anyone and everyone from the time of its announcement until the prophecy's fulfilment, which will be after the tribulation. Therefore, "The curse goes out over the face of the whole land" (Zech. 5:3) and targets every corrupt person and practice today in the same way the angel referred to those dealing in corruption, then. However, the latter is greater, reserved for the tribulation where, "The lid is lifted" (Zech. 5:9). In the same way, the curse chased, caught, and killed Judah's ancestors (Zech. 1:4-6), it will again for the current generation during the time of trouble (cf. Jer. 30:7).

Noteworthy, the reference to the "Whole land" (Zech. 5:3) refers specifically to Israel, from where Jesus will return. Just before He does, He will strike the "Shepherd" (Zech. 13:7) and the "Land" (Zech. 13:8) where, "Two thirds shall be cut off and perish, and one third shall be left alive" (Zech. 13:8). During the time of tribulation, God will save one-third of His people through the fire, purposed to test and refine them, from where they will call on His name (Zech. 13:9, Matt. 23:39). One-third of the Jews going into the tribulation, from the land, will be saved, yet still, only representing a remnant by comparison (Rom. 9:27). The people in the land will be destroyed, and the land will also be apart from Jerusalem itself (Zech. 14:10).

Within the passage, the Land is both literal (Zech. 5:3) and symbolic (Zech. 5:11). Zechariah's vision reveals that a House (temple, or dwelling place) in Babylon would be rebuilt (Zech. 5:11). However, Isaiah confirms that Babylon will never be reinhabited (Isa. 13:20), implying it will never be a world power again; therefore, future Babylon refers to a religious and political world system (Rev. 17-18). Israel came out of Babylon around 500 B.C, purposed by God to rebuild the temple. While the people of God came out of Babylon, Babylon never went out of them, which is just as accurate for many in the church today who have not come out of the world. Within Babylon, a House will be built. The house is probably the tribulation temple; therefore, Babylon is the religious and political system of the coming antichrist, who rules from Jerusalem during the second half of the tribulation (Dan. 7, 2 Thess. 2, Rev. 13).

Apart from the direct link of the "Land" (Zech. 5:3, 6, Rev. 17:3-5), further linkage is made with the "Woman" (Zech. 5:7) to Revelation chapter seventeen, which reintroduces Jezebel (Rev. 17:3). Jezebel is first mentioned in chapter two of John's revelation, in the letter from Jesus to the church of Thyatira (Rev. 2:18-29). The warning to the church of Thyatira is that unless they repent of following Jezebel, Jesus will throw them into the great tribulation (Rev. 2:22). The sin of Jezebel was sexual immorality and false worship (Rev. 2:20), resulting from watering down God's law. Jezebel was antinomian, meaning, against the law, also referring to a person who believes that Christians are released by grace from the obligation of observing the moral law, otherwise known as hyper-grace teachings. Hyper-grace teachers state that a believer can do whatever they like, and it will still be alight. In other words, they promote the false doctrine of once saved, always saved.

In Revelation, chapter seventeen, Jezebel is seen as no different, teaching lies and defiling pure worship. Again, she stands against the law of God (Rev. 17:1-3) and those who follow it (Rev. 17:2, 6, 18:24). Her attire (Rev. 17:4) is also interesting and strikingly like that of a Roman Catholic priest with their robes and adornments, who are likewise responsible for the death of millions. Historic Protestant writers often claim that the Papacy has killed fifty million or more people. Computations of fifty million killed were accepted by Voltaire, among others, and approximately covered the period from 350 A.D. to 1750 A.D. thus, the church of Rome is drunk with the blood of the martyrs (Rev. 17:2, 6). However, the end-time religious system is more significant than the Roman Catholic Church, being an ecumenical religious system inclusive of all. Albeit, the Pope will probably be its leader, taking up the position of the false prophets, or second beast, causing everyone to worship the first who is the antichrist (Rev. 13:11-18).

Towards the end of the tribulation, the antichrist and the false prophet turn against Jezebel, the great prostitute, killing her, who is the, "Great city (system) having dominion over the kings of the earth" (Rev. 17:15-18). As mentioned earlier, Jezebel represents both a religious and a political system, a one-world religion and a new world order (Rev. 17:9-12).

In sum, Zechariah's prophetic vision refers to the judgement after the tribulation period. Therefore, Revelation, chapters seventeen and eighteen, need to be further explored to gain a fuller understanding of what the judgement will look like. These chapters describe the conclusion of the time of trouble, where Jesus, on His return, will judge the world, not just the land of Israel. When Jesus returns, He will consider every corrupt religious and political practice, putting an end to it once and for all.

Many will come to faith in Jesus during the tribulation, including the Jews (Zech. 12:10-13:1, 8-9, 14:16, Rom. 11:25-32, Rev. 7, 14). Likewise, will many from the lukewarm church (Rev. 3:14-22), who did not repent before the rapture and were, therefore, 'left behind.' Through the hour of trial (Rev. 3:10), the left behind will come to true and lasting faith, through repentance, in Jesus, which is the purpose of the tribulation; to bring about salvation through repentance, through fire.

At the commencement of the millennium, before establishing the Messianic kingdom, God will remove everything false (Zech. 5:9-11, 14:20-21). During the millennial dispensation, the one who once prophesied falsely will even lie to cover his shame (Zech. 13:1-6). The dreamers and diviners who afflicted God's people, against whom God's anger is hot (Zech. 10:2). The false prophets are one in the same, "Swearing falsely" (Zech. 5:4), leading many astray (Zech. 10:3) in pursuit of their own greedy gain (Zech. 11:3), causing the whole land to be full of iniquity (Zech. 5:6).

In the same way, many are deceived today. Many more believers will be caught up in Babylon during the tribulation, hence the call to, "Come out of her" (Rev. 18:4). God is calling His people out of the world now and will do again throughout the time of trouble, just before destroying the Babylonian system once and for all. When Babylon is destroyed, the saints will then sing, "No more for your merchants (including religious leaders and institutions such as the Roman Catholic Church) were the great ones of the earth, and all nations were deceived by your sorcery, and in her was found the blood of the prophets and the saints, and of all who have been slain in earth" (Rev. 18:23-24).

In conclusion, what John recorded through the book of Revelation, the prophet Zechariah wrote referring to swift judgement coming upon the land, and the earth announced through the flying scroll. What John describes in Revelation, chapter eighteen, will be the fulfilment of Zechariah's prophecy, the false and the thieves will be cleaned out, once and for all (Zech. 5:3). Yes, they will be forever removed (Zech. 5:4). Revelation, chapters twenty-one (vv. 8, 27) and twenty-two (v. 15) repeat the warning, referring to the new world where nothing unclean will enter. Like with the temple (Zech. 2:1-2) and the scroll (Zech. 5:2), the new city is precisely measured (Rev. 21:15-19), as will the people entering, weighed up for good or for bad (cf. Prov. 16:2, Dan. 5:27, 1 Cor. 3:13, Rev. 20:11-15).

CHAPTER SIX—PART ONE

THE FOUR CHARIOTS

'Impatience to Go and Patrol the Earth'
(Zech. 6:1-8)

Chapter six of the book of Zechariah reintroduces the four chariots through the eighth vision given to the prophet. The imagery of chapter six takes us back to chapter one, linked with the red and the white horse patrolling the earth (Zech. 1:7-8). The first and eighth visions, containing the same imagery, essentially serve as bookends with everything else sandwiched in between. In the last vision, the four chariots are drawn by red, black, white, and dappled horses (Zech. 6:2) who patrol the earth (Zech. 6:7, cf. 1:10-11). The horses present themselves before God (Zech. 6:5, cf. 1:11) and appear from between two "Bronze mountains" (Zech. 6:1-2), representing judgment on the Gentile nations, North and South (Zech. 6:6). In chapter one, the horses first appeared in a valley among the myrtle trees (Zech. 1:8).

Myrtle is symbolic of the recovery and the establishment of God's promises (Isa. 41:19, 55:13). Like the four horses sent by God (Zech. 1:10), the four chariots, led by horses, are also like those seen in the book of Revelation (Rev. 6:1-8), which are released by God (Rev. 6:1). The four chariots are also the four winds (Zech. 6:5) and are arguably the same as those mentioned in Daniel's book (Dan. 7:2).

As mentioned above, the Bronze mountains represent judgement, the righteous judgement of the Lord (cf. Rev. 1:15; 2:18). There are two well-known mountains within scripture, mainly through prophetic literature, 1). Mount Zion (Joel 3:16) and 2). The Mount of Olives (Zech. 14:4). Mount Zion is where God dwells, or at least will (Ps. 74:2, Isa. 8:18), and the Mount of Olives is where Jesus returns to (Zech. 14:4). The Mount of Olives is also the location where Jesus taught the "Olivet Discord" (Matt. 24, Mk. 13, Lu. 21). The Olivet discord reveals the things to come, preceding the return of Jesus Christ, narrowing in on the temple (Matt. 24:15), as does Zechariah's vision, albeit they are two different temples (Zech. 6:12-15). The temple Jesus indirectly refers to is the third tribulation temple (Matt. 24:15), and the latter is the millennial temple (cf. Mal. 3:1).

Before the millennial temple is built, the chariots (spirits) are sent to the north and the south around the time the tribulation temple is built. The application is universal judgement, patrolling the earth (Zech. 6:7, cf. 1:10), where God is, "Exceedingly angry with the nations that are at ease" (Zech. 1:15). For a time, God allows the nations to trouble Israel (Zech. 1:18-19); at the end of the tribulation, He will shake (Hag. 2:22), terrify and cast them down (Zech. 1:21).

In chapter one, the four horses of Zechariah report that, "All the earth remains at rest" (Zech. 1:11), like chapter six, verse eight. However, the difference between the two accounts is before and after judgement. After the judgement, "The Lord of all the earth" (Zech. 6:5) is known to all because He is the visible ruling Messiah.

Again, the winds (Zech. 6:5), or God's messengers (Ps. 104:4), are blown in the directions of the north, and the south yet are told to patrol the earth (Zech. 6:7-8). God accomplishes His will through these spirits influencing men (2 Thess. 2:11, Rev. 17:17). From where Zechariah is standing, the north is Babylon, and the south is Egypt, representing sin. The New Testament often uses Babylon as the symbolic place of evil, also referred to as Rome (Rev. 17:7–18). Examples of Babylon used as a symbol of sin are numerous within the book of Revelation (Rev. 14:8, 16:19, 17:5, 18:2, 18:10, and 18:21). Revelation, chapter seventeen (v. 5), is an excellent example of Babylon as a metaphor for sin, like chapter eleven (v. 8) for Egypt. Peter also used the Babylonian metaphor for sin (1 Pet. 5:13).

The point and purpose of the chariots are that they go out to deal with sin by executing God's divine wrath (Zech. 5:5-11, 6:5). Like with the previous visions, the prophesied judgement in chapter six of Zechariah's book is set and reserved for the end of time, the coming tribulation period (Rev. 18:2, 10, 21; 19:1–3).

As mentioned earlier, the judgement of Zechariah's first vision on the Gentiles (Zech. 1:15) is seen again in the second vision (Zech. 1:20-22) and is satisfied in the last (Zech. 6:8). After the judgement has been poured out in full (Rev. 14:10), and the wrath of God is finished (Rev. 15:1, 16:17, 19:2, 15-19), then, and not before, there will be rest (Zech. 6:8) which is lasting peace. Further support for this statement is seen in the following verses (Zech. 6:9-15), symbolically referring to Jesus Christ, the Branch, who builds the millennial temple, then rules and reigns from it.

It is important to note with the coming judgement, that God sets the appointed times (Act 17:26). He is in complete control over every matter (1 Pet. 4:17, Rev. 20:12-13), which includes the tribulation itself (Isa. 26:9). The evidence of God being in control over the tribulation events is seen where even the angel (winds) must present themselves to Him before being sent and unleashed on the earth (Zech. 1:10, 6:5, Rev. 6:5). The release of the four chariots (Zech. 6:2), led by the white, red, black, and pale horses (cf. Rev. 6:1-8), will finalise God's judgements over the entire population of the planet (cf. Rev. 19:2, 15–19), before resting in Babylon (Zech. 6:8, cf. 5:9-11, Rev. 18). Again, the rest (peace of God) following the judgement (Zech. 6:8) follows the utter destruction of the corrupt world and religious system (Zech. 5:8-11), taking place in a single day (Rev. 18:8), and in a single hour (Rev. 18:10, 17, 19), after the seven-year ordeal (Dan. 9:20-27).

To better understand what the judgment entails, an examination of Revelation chapter six, compared with Matthew, chapter twenty-four, needs to be undertaken. As mentioned earlier, Matthew's account of the Olivet Discord (Matt. 24) is connected to the two mountains, symbolic of judgement (Zech. 6:1).

Through the Olivet discord, Jesus foretold and forewarned of the same events John saw and recorded through the book of Revelation, chapter six, when asked: "What will be the signs of your coming and the close of the age?" (Matt. 24:4). In response, Jesus warned of coming, and increasing deception (Matt. 24: 5, 11, 24). He is referring to the white horse (Rev. 6:2), followed by war (Matt. 24:6-7, 22) which is the red horse (Rev. 6:3-4), then famine (Matt. 24:7b-8) being the black horse (Rev. 6:5-6) and lastly, pestilence/sickness (Matt. 24.7, cf. Luke 21:11) which is the pale horse (Rev. 6.7-8). These horses (winds) will not only be an 'opening event' for the tribulation but will be an ongoing concern from the start of the ordeal until the end. Moreover, the four apocalyptic horsemen are a continuous instrument of judgment throughout the time of trouble, seen through the seals (Rev. 6, 8:1-5), trumpets (Rev. 8:6-9:1-21, 11:1-19), and bowls (Rev. 16).

To qualify, the white horse represents the antichrist, revealed on the signing of the peace treaty (Isa. 28:15, 18), triggering the tribulation (Dan. 9:20-27, 2 Thess. 2:1-12). The antichrist will be a great deceiver, operating with the activity of Satan, with all power and false signs and wonders (2

Thess. 2:9, Rev. 13:13-14). He will deceive many, even those confessing Christ (Matt. 24:24), into following and worshiping him. So deceptive will he be that God had to cut the tribulation days short, least none be left on His return (Matt. 24:22). On this note, it is essential to clarify; that the tribulation elect (Matt. 24:22) refers to those in the tribulation who have been 'left behind'. The left behind have missed the rapture (1 Cor. 15:51-52, 1 Thess. 5:2-10, especially v. 9, Rev. 3:10, 4:1).

The rapture of the saints occurs at the commencement of the tribulation, for the antichrist cannot be revealed until after the church has first been removed (2 Thess. 2:3-6). Furthermore, the signing of the Middle East Peace Treaty will take place after the church has been removed, for that also reveals the identity of the antichrist (Isa. 28:15, 18, Dan. 9:24-27). The antichrist is the one signing off on the covenant of death. The book of Revelation (chapters 13, 14, 16, 19, and 20) describes the antichrist's activity and judgment.

Following the white horse is the red horse, representing war (Rev. 6:4). War is a constant and increasing theme throughout the tribulation. It is likely a war (Ps. 83, Isa. 17) will be the catalyst for signing the Middle East Peace Treaty, triggering the "Hour of trial" (Rev. 3:10) in the same way as the Six-Day War or Yom Kippur War motivated the semi-successful signing of the Oslo Accords. Accordingly, "The red horse is permitted to take peace from the earth, so men should slay one another, and he [is] given a great sword" (Rev. 6:4). The best portrayal of this is seen in Revelation, chapter nine (vv. 15-16), describing an army numbering two hundred million. These will kill a third of humanity (Rev. 9:15, 18). The army comprises horses and mounted troops (Rev. 9:16), who are under the influence of four powerful demons (Rev. 9:14-15). Joel (chapter 2) also addressed this future army of super-soldiers. Nothing like them has even been seen before or will be again (Joel 2:2). However, like every other judgement, God is in complete control and is the one releasing the angels (winds), who are growing impatient (Zech. 6:7), prepared for this very day and hour (Rev. 9:15), to bring men to repentance (Rev. 9:20-21).

The army of two hundred million is most likely China and company, confirmed by Revelation, chapter sixteen (v. 12), stating they are the, "Kings of the East" (cf. Dan. 11:40-45). As with Revelation, chapter nine (vv. 20-21), following the judgements designed to bring about repentance, a repeat occurs in chapter sixteen, where humanity refuses to repent (Rev. 16:9-10). The same is also seen in chapter six, following the release of the four apocalyptic horsemen (Rev. 6:12-17).

Like the four horses (Rev. 6:1-8), the kings of the east will operate with great supernatural power (Rev. 16:14), gathering to participate in the greatest war this planet has ever seen, or will again, the battle of Armageddon. (Rev. 16:14-16). The battle of Armageddon will complete the tribulation when Jesus returns (Rev. 19:11-21), only then resulting in lasting peace (Zech. 6:8).

The black horse (Rev. 6:5) represents famine following the red horse. Due to the ongoing war, natural catastrophe, chaos, and other various plagues, the tribulation will see an unprecedented level of deficiency of food levels. Accordingly, it will take a whole day's wages to purchase the poorest and most humble meals (Rev. 6:6). So severe will the famine be that even the wild animals turn on humankind as a source of food (Rev. 6:8b). Due to the shortage of food, the tribulation population will likewise go to any length to secure supplies, including robbery and murder.

The coming tribulation can only be described as a dangerous time fueled by extreme hunger and desperation. Adding to the mix of the black horse and the red horse is the pale horse, where war, pestilence, and famine are combined (Rev. 6:8). The pale horse represents disease, sweeping hundreds of millions into hell. As a result of these plagues, a fourth of the world's population will be killed, which will equate to around two billion people. So effective and severe are these horse riders that Death and Hades follow them (Rev. 6:8).

In sum, the above described and detailed level of death and destruction will be a continuing theme throughout the tribulation, climaxing with Jesus' return, which is why He said, "There has never been a time like it, and never will be again" (Matt. 24:21, cf. Jer. 30:7, Dan. 12:1). As mentioned before, every judgement, whether it falls under the seals (Rev. 6, 8:1-5), trumpets (Rev. 8:6-9:1-21, 11:1-19), or bowls (Rev. 16), it is connected to the four-horse riders of the apocalypse. The combined judgments will wipe out most of the planet's remaining population. Only a remnant by comparison to today's population will survive the seven-year tribulation ordeal, never mind the concluding battle of Armageddon (Rev. 19:11-21). Only those surviving and submitting to Jesus will enter the millennial kingdom (God's rest, e.g., Zech. 6:8, 14:16) to repopulate the earth.

Today, we are experiencing the beginning of the "Things to come" (Col. 2:17), just as Jesus predicted two thousand years ago, we would. When asked for the signs of the close of the age (Matt. 24:3), Jesus summarised the above-mentioned, saying, "These are the beginning of birth pains" (Matt. 24:8). In other words, they will be evident before the tribulation period is due to commence. Fulfilling prophecy, these signs are now plain and increasing. These signs of the times indicate that the close of the age is here, and Jesus' return is near (Lu. 21:28).

CHAPTER SIX—PART TWO

THE BRANCH AND THE TEMPLE

'The Coming, Crowned King'
(Zech. 6:9-15)

The introduction of the word, succeeding the visions, is found in other places, "The word of the Lord came to me" (Zech. 4:8, 7:4, 8:1, 18). The visions and words prophesy future events, communicated symbolically through the visions and literally through the words. The word of chapter six (vv. 9-15) commences with known people to the prophet, who have come out of Babylon (Zech. 6:10). Specifically, Joshua, the high priest, is the focus who is crowned (Zech. 6:11). Interestingly, Joshua is crowned, not Zerubbabel the governor (Hag. 1:1, 12, 14; 2:21; cf. Zech. 4:6–10). Zerubbabel was a descendant of King David; therefore, if he were crowned, some would have mistaken him to be the Messianic King, such as Daniel was expecting at the end of the Babylonian captivity and empire (Dan. 9). On the other hand, Joshua signifies a future king as a Branch type (Zech. 6:12, cf. 3:8). The Branch and the future king would be like the priestly king, Melchizedek, seen centuries earlier (Gen.

14:18–20; Ps. 110:4; cf. Heb. 7:11–21). The term Branch points to Jesus, the Messiah, and the coming King of kings, succeeding the antichrist.

The eighth vision indirectly introduced the antichrist, who is the white horse, leading three others, as seen through the book of Revelation (Rev. 6:1-8). After the tribulation, another white horse appears - Jesus (Rev. 19:11-21), who deals with the first. Following the judgement of the antichrist, the prophet looks further ahead to the, "Crowning of the Branch" (Zech. 6:11-12). Again, the Branch type is Joshua (Zech. 6:11), symbolic of Jesus (Zech. 3:8). Therefore, the message of the latter half of Zechariah, chapter six, is that Jesus, the Branch, will rule as the crowned King from the rebuilt millennial temple (Isa. 9:7; Jer. 23:5; Micah 4:3, 7; Zeph. 3:15; Zech. 14:9).

The task of rebuilding the second temple was assigned to Zerubbabel (Zech. 4:9); however, Joshua is the focus of this section, concluding that rebuilding the second temple is connected to the last. The Branch will build the last and millennial temple (Zech. 6:12-13), which follows the third. Again, the Branch is Christ, clothed in royal honour (Zech. 6:13, Isa. 4:2), ruling from the temple (Zech. 6:13) as King and Priest in the order of Melchizedek (Heb. 4:15; 5:6; 7:11–21).

Important to note, like Zechariah's eight visions, the words received leap two-thousand five hundred years into the future. The fulfilment of the prophetic vision occurs post-tribulation, where the last temple will be built at the commencement of the millennium (Zech. 6:13, cf. Isa. 2:2–4; 56:6–7; Ezek. 40–46; Micah 4:1–2). Alongside Jesus, people from many nations in the millennial world will contribute, bringing their wealth for the temple rebuild (Zech. 6:15, Isa. 60:5, 9, 11; 61:6b; Hag. 2:7–8), repeating that of Solomon's day, contributing joyfully to the reconstruction (cf. 2 Kings, 12:4, 1 Chron. 29:9). Remember, only those surviving the tribulation

(Zech. 14:16), who "Diligently obey the voice of the Lord" (Zech. 6:15), will participate in the temple rebuild.

Before the millennial temple can be built, one more must first stand in the way: the third tribulation temple. One of the most evident signs of the times and indicators of Jesus' imminent return is the rebuilding of the third temple. Today, a great deal of discussion in Jerusalem concerning its reconstruction is taking place. Much planning has been carried out to gather materials and artifacts, including the Ark of the Covenant. Furthermore, the re-establishment of Levitical training to conduct temple rituals and sacrifices. Replica temples have also been built off-site in preparation for the real thing. The tribulation temple is predicted to be rebuilt during the seven years of trouble (Dan. 9:24–27; Matt. 24:15–16; 2 Thess. 2:3-4; Rev. 11:1-2; 13:15). The completion of which falls somewhere within the first forty-two months (Rev. 11:2), allowing for the prophesied, "Abomination of desolation" (Matt. 24:15) to be fulfilled (cf. Dan. 9:27), triggering the great tribulation (Matt. 24:21). The location of such is presumed to be upon the temple mount where the two previous temples once stood. From there, the 'Abomination of desolation' is fulfilled where the antichrist announces that he is God (2 Thess. 2:4).

Chapter thirteen of the book of Revelation provides further detail about this event. The abomination of desolation will include the setting up of an idol (the antichrist) who will cause outrage amongst God-fearing Jews, resulting in immediate and immense persecution (cf. Matt. 24:16-22; Rev. 12:13-17; 13:7). Remember, many call themselves Jews who are not (Rev. 2:9, 3:9). The Jews who are false are those promoting and following a false religion in pursuit of a false messiah. These false Jews (religious type) have troubled both Israel and the church; however, the day is coming when they too must acknowledge and submit to Jesus Christ (cf. Isa. 45:23; Rom. 14:11; Phil. 2:10–11). Not only the Jews but also every other persecutor of the saints, for Jesus said, "I will make them come and fall at your feet and acknowledge that I have loved you" (Rev. 3:9). But until then, the false (including Catholics and Muslims) will continue to trouble God's people, even escalating their persecution before and during the tribulation.

Around the latter half of the tribulation, Jerusalem will become desolate following the abomination of desolation due to the remaining Israelites fleeing into the wilderness (Matt. 24:15) to a place God has prepared (Mk. 13:14: Rev. 12:6), hence the desolation. The (real) Jews will remain in the wilderness for one thousand two hundred and sixty days (Rev. 12:6, 14), which is the latter part of the tribulation. As mentioned earlier, the entire tribulation period lasts seven years. In the second three-and-a-half-year period of the tribulation, the antichrist will be fully empowered by Satan (Dan. 7:25; 2 Thess. 2:9; Rev. 13:5) following his resurrection, for he, "Was, and is not, and is about to rise from the bottomless pit and go into destruction" (Rev. 17:8, 11, cf. 11:7, 13:3, 12, 14). The antichrist will be killed just before the great tribulation commences (Matt. 24:21), which is the second half, rising from the bottomless pit, performing great signs and wonders (Rev. 13:13). The resurrection itself will be a great sign and wonder. Through this resurrection miracle, many will be deceived. When Satan is cast to the earth at the midpoint of the tribulation (Rev. 12:7-8, 13), he gives the antichrist his power (2 Thess. 2:9).

After the construction of the third temple, God will reach out to the people of Israel through the two witnesses who preach Christ crucified (1 Cor. 1:23), the resurrected One, who reappeared (1 Cor. 15:1-6) and ascended to heaven, and who will soon, return (Acts 1:9-12). The two witnesses will preach "The gospel" for the latter forty-two months of the tribulation (Rev. 11:2-3). As mentioned in Zechariah, chapter four, they will have supernatural power like Moses and Elijah. Again, many today speculate over who the two witnesses will be, yet Moses and Elijah appear to have the most substantial support.

Tim Lahaye provides the following - "Proponents of the Moses and Elijah argument point out that these two Old Testament characters were the most influential Hebrew men of their times. Moses introduced God's written Law to Israel, while Elijah was the first of the writing prophets and even started the school of the prophets. Whenever the Jews said, "Moses and Elijah," they usually meant, "the Law and the Prophets."

One factor that may suggest that Moses and Elijah will be the two witnesses mentioned in Revelation is that the two men accompanied Jesus at the Transfiguration (Matt. 17). Another element is that the miracles the witnesses are to produce have striking similarities to the judgement plagues initiated by Moses and Elijah in the Old Testament (see Exod. 7-12; and 1 Kgs. 17:1).

After the two witnesses' ministry is complete, the beast (antichrist) will be given the power to destroy them (Rev. 11:7). The two witnesses will lay dead in the street for three days before being resurrected (Rev. 11:11). Their resurrection is visible to all, as will be their ascension (rapture) into heaven (Rev. 11:12), causing those who heard and received their message of the true Messiah to fear and give glory to God (Rev. 11:13). The resurrection of the two witnesses will counter the resurrection of the antichrist. Both the true and the false will be doing great signs and wonders throughout the tribulation, only to be dwarfed by the greatest end times sign, the return of Jesus Christ (Matt. 24:30).

After the tribulation, as the third temple is utterly defiled by the proclamation and deeds of the antichrist, that is the abomination of desolation (Dan. 9:27; 2 Thess. 2:4; Rev. 13:3-7), it will be destroyed. The destruction of the tribulation will occur during the forty-five-day interval, taking place between the tribulation and the millennial/Messianic Kingdom (Dan.

12:12). At the millennial temple's establishment, there was also an interval lasting thirty days (Dan. 12:11). The thirty-day gap marks the midpoint of the tribulation, separating the tribulation from the great tribulation (Matt. 24:21). The great tribulation is like a time never seen before (Jer. 30:7, Dan. 12:1, cf. Joel 2:2). Anyone surviving the latter half of the trial and who is found waiting for the Messiah's return is considered "Blessed" (Dan. 12:12a). However, the book of Revelation says, those who die early during the great tribulation are blessed (Rev. 14:13). In other words, the lucky ones die early.

In sum, the tribulation period will be like a time never seen before, with great signs and wonders deceiving most. So deceptive will this time be, even God's elect, if possible, would be led astray (Matt. 24:24). However, the greatest of the end time signs will be the return of Jesus (Matt. 24:30). When Jesus returns, He will destroy the tribulation temple and replace it with the millennial temple (Zech. 6:12-13a). However, the millennial temple will not so much be built by man but will Descend from heaven, like with the latter new city (Rev. 21:3). During the millennium, the new city and temple will remain aloft over Jerusalem (Zech. 14:10).

Following Christ's return and during the forty-five-day interval, Jesus, and the saints, will prepare the survivors of the tribulation (Zech. 14:16) for millennial worship (Zech. 14:16-21), as also prophesied by Ezekiel (Ezek. 40:5- 43:27). During the seventh dispensation, a millennial system of priesthood and sacrifice will be reinstituted, resembling something of the commandments concerning the Law of Moses. Ezekiel deals with this subject, providing a detailed account covering two chapters of his book (Ezek. 44:1-46 and 45:1-25). One of the prominent features mentioned in Ezekiel's prophecy of the futuristic millennial temple will be the return of God's shekinah glory (Ezek. 44:4-8) - essentially the return of God's very presence and being. Until now, despite many claims, we have not and will not see the shekinah glory of God. It will, however, return during the millennial dispensation because Jesus, the Crowned Branch, is ruling and reigning from the temple, which is God's dwelling place.

During the millennial dispensation, it is said that King David will rule and reign as the righteous Branch (Isa. 9:7, Jer. 23:5, 30:9). Second Samuel (7:16) supports the idea, saying David's throne will endure forever. Ezekiel states that during the millennial reign, king David will ensure the nations keep the commands of God (Ezek. 37:24). While on the earth, David was both king, and priest, sometimes referred to as the priestly king (1 Chron. 15:25-27, 17:27). However, all believers are called kings and priests (Rev. 1:6, 2:26-27, 3:21, 5:10, 11:15, 20:4, cf. 1 Cor. 6:2, 1 Pet. 2:9). When Jesus returns to the earth with the saints to execute judgement (Jude 14), David will be among them, called to co-ruling (Dan. 7:27). However, Jesus, the Son of David (Matt. 15:22, 21:9, Mk. 10:48, 12:35), will rule (Lu. 1:32), not the literal David.

Sometimes Jesus is referred to as David, causing confusion, in the same way, John the Baptist was called Elijah (Mal. 4:5, Lu. 1:17, Mk. 9:11-13). Jesus is David's descendant (Jn. 7:42, Rom. 1:3, 2 Tim. 2:8, Rev. 5:5); both David and Jesus are in the order of Melchizedek. However, the righteous Branch given to David (Jer. 23:5, 33:9) will rule in the millennium. In sum, David will rule through Jesus, as all believers will. Through Christ, believers will reign (2 Tim. 2:11-13). In this life, faithful followers reign over their sin (Rom. 5:17), and in the next, they will reign over nations. The ten minors' parable confirms that faithful followers will reign over nations (Lu. 19:11-27). During the millennial dispensation, the saints, who, "Diligently obeyed the voice of the Lord" (Zech. 6:15), will be given levels of authority in the kingdom according to how they handle God's responsibilities in this age (Lu. 19:17). However, Jesus, the "Crowned Branch," will be the Head, with the global government on His shoulders (Isa. 9:6).

REBUILD THE TEMPLE

'Diligent Obedience (Zech. 6:16),
Results in Prosperity (Ezra 5:8, 6:14)'
(Ezra 5-6)

Chronologically following Zachariah, chapter six, which is focused on the last millennial temple, springboarding from the second (Zech. 4:6-10) is Ezra's account. Ezra reintroduces the prophets Haggai and Zechariah, who encourage Judah to stay the course (Ezra 5:1-2). Again, Haggai's prophecy also springboarded from the second temple to the last (Hag. 2), where, "The latter glory will be greater than the former" (Hag. 2:9). Zechariah did the same, stating, "The Branch (Jesus) will be crowned" (Zech. 6:11-12). The anticipation of the second temple was that it would usher in the Messiah (the Branch). The issue that the prophet Haggai addressed was that Judah had stopped building the temple, saying, "The time has not yet come to rebuild the house of the Lord" (Hag. 1:2), despite being told to do so by the king (Ezra 1:2-4).

Taken from the previous section given to Haggai of this work, a reminder of the following is repeated, After arriving in Jerusalem in the first year of Darius' reign, the Jews got to work rebuilding the temple, starting with the alter, recommencing sacrifices in the Holy Land (Ezra 3:1-6). Following the building of the altar, in the second year of arrival, the Jews began rebuilding the temple (Ezra 3:1-17). Everyone was involved in the project (Ezra 3:8) - yet not all were pleased with the progress when comparing the second temple with the first (Ezra 3:12, Hag. 2:3, Zech. 4:10). Furthermore, not everyone was happy with the project, for the enemies of Judah attempted to interfere with the progress through trickery, bribes, and threats (Ezra 4:1-5). Judah's enemies were victorious for a time, stopping the assignment (Ezra 4:24-5:1). The work stopped until Darius succeeded Cyrus.

At that time, the prophets Haggai and Zechariah prophesied to the Jews in Jerusalem (Ezra 5:1). On the third year back in the Land, Haggai received a word from the Lord, addressing the Jews who claimed, "The time has not yet come to rebuild the house of the Lord" (Hag. 1:2). The temple remained in ruins while the high priests lived in luxury (Hag. 1:1-4, 9). In pursuit of prosperity (Hag. 1:9b), the Jews abandoned God's work in favour of their own, yet to no avail. No matter what they did to fill their pockets, whatever went in, came out just as fast (Hag. 1:5-6). Whatever the Jews could acquire, God blew it away (Hag. 1:9a). Judah's neglect brought God's correction through the prophet, "Consider your ways!" (Hag. 1:5, 7), and "Rebuild My house!" (Hag. 1:8).

The repeat of the above-mentioned is essential to establish some framework for the following chapters of Ezra (5-6). The background also reminds the reader that when considering the prophetic last temple through the visions, the prophets are excited about the second yet see something of the fourth, albeit two thousand, five hundred years into the future, unbeknownst to them. It is doubtful the prophets discerned the difference between the two.

To reiterate, the background for Ezra, chapters five and six springboards off Zechariah chapters four and six, and the book of Haggai, where the work of the temple had stopped (Ezra 4:1-5, 24, Hag. 1). Through the influence of the prophets, Haggai and Zechariah, the work recommenced and continued until finished (Ezra 5:1-2), as a result, the Jews prospered (Ezra 5:8, 6:14). Again, both prophets focused on the finished work of the temple, pointing to the future glory of God (Hag. 2:9, Zech. 6:13). Therefore, the importance of the project points to the preparation necessary for the coming King, Jesus. Namely, the positioning and readiness of God's people through obedience (Zech. 6:15). A glimpse and foreshadowing of the positional reward is seen in Ezra, chapter six (v. 21).

The problem with the temple not being completed is that the worship requirement would not be met. Judah would stray without the practice of pure worship, which was evident through Haggai's writings (Hag. 1:4-6). Instead, Judah has strayed, chasing their own interests, over God's. Instead of fearing God and remaining obedient to Him, they pursued prosperity. As mentioned earlier, Judah got off track due to outside interference through trickery, bribes, and threats (Ezra 4:1-5).

Unlike Haggai's need to challenge Judah when troubled, Ezra praised them, stating the elders fixed their eyes on God, who, "Did not stop" building (Ezra 5:5). Haggai mentioned outside interference caused the initial problem, while Ezra dives deeper into who was interfering and how the issue was resolved. The troublemakers on this account were Tattenai and Shethar-bozenai and their associates (Ezra 5:6, 6:6). Tattenai and Shethar-bozenai were leaders that governed neighbouring lands "Beyond the river" (Ezra 5:3, 6). The temple rebuild was perceived as a direct threat to Judah's neighbours, who believed Judah was rebelling against the Persian empire. The evidence is seen when they asked, "Who gave you a decree to build the house and finish this structure?" (Ezra 5:3, 9). The 'House' refers to the temple. Remember in Zechariah, chapter five (vv. 4, 11), the woman in the basket was flown from the House in Israel to the House in Babylon. The suggestion is from the second temple to the third. Babylon is symbolic of the world system and the new world order to come. The meaning of Zechariah, chapter five is that the limited defilement of the second temple will be unlimited in the third tribulation temple.

Adding to the first question, another followed, "What are the names of the men who are building this building?" (Ezra 5:4, cf. v. 10). Again, unlike Haggai's account, Judah's leaders held fast this time, fixing their eyes on God, who had His eyes set on them. Unlike their forefathers, with whom God was angry (Ezra 5:12, Zech. 1:2), and the initial failure when commencing the temple rebuild, this time, the elders did not consider man or themselves (Ezra 5:5). Again, in the previous attempt, the prophet Haggai rebuked them by saying, "Consider your ways" (Hag. 1:6, 7). Now, due to having considered their ways and having returned to God (Zech. 1:3), God was watching over Judah (Ezra. 5:1, 5), who were fearfully and faithfully committed to Him (Hag. 1:12-14). Because they feared and obeyed God, and not man, despite opposition, "The hand of the LORD was on them" (cf. Ezra 7:6, 9, 28; 8:18, 22, 31; Neh. 2:8, 18).

As mentioned earlier, Ezra dives deeper into the activities of the troublemakers, providing insights into what takes place behind the scenes, narrowing in on Tattenai, who sent a tell-tale letter to Darius (Ezra 5:6-16). Of interest is Tattenai's reference to God as, "The great God" (Ezra 5:8) who was previously proclaimed to be great by Darius (Dan. 6:20, 25-27). Nebuchadnezzar did the same (Dan. 4:1-3, 34-35), separating them from their pagan beliefs.

In the same way, God set Israel and those who joined them, apart from the other gods (Ezra 5:11, 6:21), making a distinguishing difference between them and the other nations. Due to separation and obedience, the people of God prospered (Ezra 5:8, 6:14), as promised (Hag. 2).

In the same way, the promise of destruction was previously fulfilled (Ezra 5:12, Zech. 1:2, 4-5) - the promise of prosperity was. Again, the origin of the promises in Deuteronomy (28, 30:11-20). God destroyed Judah through His servant Nebuchadnezzar (Jer. 25:9; 27:6; 43:10), and He was now prospering them through His servant Cyrus (Isa. 41:1 44: 28, Ezra 5:13-17). In Ezra's writings, King Cyrus is a prominent and instrumental figure referenced twelve times from chapters one to six.

In response to Tattenai's letter and request that the records be searched (Ezra 6:1, cf. 5:17), a scroll was found (Ezra 6:2), confirming that King Cyrus had issued a decree (Ezra 6:3, 14, cf. 1:2-4) concerning the house (temple) of God. Interestingly, the scroll was found three hundred miles away from Babylon, being Ecbatana (Ezra 6:2). Once found, the king confirmed the decree to Tattenai, telling him to keep away and leave the Jews alone (Ezra 6:6-7), then adding to help the Jews (Ezra 6:8). The king's decree was reinforced with a threat of death; if anyone interferes with the temple rebuild, their house will be ruined, and they would be impaled (Ezra 6:11-12).

Again, through the king's verdict, Darius confirmed God as the God of heaven, the great God (Ezra 5:8), even coveting the prayers of the Jews for himself and his sons (Ezra 6:10). By way of ensuring and protecting the hope of blessing, Darius favours the Jews, "Those who bless Israel will be blessed" (Gen. 12:3, Num. 24:9). The reverse is also true, "Those who curse Israel will be cursed." Tattenai can testify to that, now having to pay for the temple rebuild out of his own pocket, under the threat of death. Anyone who interfered with the temple now would come under the curse of Darius, which was fulfilled through Antiochus (167 B.C), who died three years after defiling the temple. The curse was also fulfilled through Herod the Great (37–4 B.C), who glorified himself through the temple's renovation, which was destroyed by the Romans (70 A.D). Herold also died of disease, but not before having his fair share of domestic troubles.

The next one to defile the temple will be the antichrist, who will also come under the curse of Darius when Jesus returns (Rev. 19:20).

Under the protection of the king, the revenue of Tattenai, and the encouragement of the prophets (Ezra 5:1), the Jews diligently built the temple (Ezra 5:8, 6:13). Collectively, the pagan kings, governors, and the Jews rebuilt God's house (Ezra 613-15). The work was completed a little over four years from when Haggai rebuked Judah, "Consider your ways" (Hag. 1:6, 7). Once finished, the temple was dedicated to God (Ezra 6:16-18); the Jews were also devoted to God, "Separating themselves from the uncleanness of the people of the land to worship the Lord, the God of Israel" (Ezra. 6:22).

The reference to the Law of Moses (Ezra 3:2, 6:18, 7:6) and the Passover sacrifice (Ezra 6:19-20) is important, due to covering them and their sin. The Passover is in remembrance of what took place in Egypt (Exod. 12). The Passover was an act of separation between the Israelites from the Egyptians (Exod. 12:21-30) in the same way it served between Judah and the Persians. The same is true today; through the blood of Christ (Jn. 1:29), the Passover Lamb (1 Cor. 5:7) separates those that are His from those that are not (Rev. 5:9-10).

As mentioned earlier, the importance of the temple rebuild was to prepare the people of God for the coming Messiah and His earthly rule (Zech. 6:9-15). The temple of the Holy Spirit serves the same purpose (1 Cor. 3:16, 6:19). Paul warns, as did Darius, "If anyone destroys God's temple, God will destroy him" (1 Cor. 3:16). In addition, Paul warns that anyone who practices sin will be destroyed (1 Cor. 6:12-18).

In the same way, Tattenai came under the threat of death for interfering with the temple. Despite his ill-will, what he meant for evil, God meant it for good (cf. Gen. 50:20). A repeat is seen through the book of Esther (480 BC), where Haman plotted against the Jews (Esther 3), resulting in his death (Esther 7). What Haman designed for Mordecai was used to kill him. Again, Tattenai was threatened by Darius with execution by impaling if he interfered with the Jews; while Tattenai avoided that fate, Haman suffered it (Ester 7:10).

In conclusion, the second temple is the platform for the third temple, as seen through Haggai's vision (Hag. 2) and Zechariah's (Zech. 4:6:9-15). Once again, God will orchestrate it. The second temple served to place the Jews, and anyone who joined them (Zech. 2:11) in right standing with God (Ezra. 6:21), and the third will do the same. However, the third temple will achieve the result differently. The second temple was the place of sacrifice for sin, and the third will be defiled by taking away the sacrifice (Dan. 11:31), replaced by the desolation of abomination (Dan. 11:32). The desolation of abomination is the proclamation of the antichrist that he is God (2 Thess. 2:4). As with Tattenai and Haman, the God of Israel will intervene on behalf of the God-fearing and obedient Jews throughout that time. During the time of trouble, God will save the Jews and anyone else who joins themselves to Him through them. On each occasion, the temple (first, second, and third) is critical for preparing and placing people in right standing before God.

CHAPTER SEVEN

FALSE WORSHIP

'Beware of Bethel'
(Zech. 7:1-14)

Following the word of the crowned Branch (Jesus) in the millennial temple (Zech. 6:9-15) comes another word (Zech. 7:1). This time, it is given nearly two years after the visions; in all, there were eight visions (Zech. 1-6). The word also comes around the halfway mark of rebuilding the temple (Zech. 7:1), which took around four years to finish after Haggai's challenge, "Consider your ways" (Hag. 1:5, 7). From Ezra, it is revealed that after departing from the temple project (Ezra 4) and being challenged by God (Hag. 1), through the prophet (Ezra 5), Judah got back on track and completed the job (Ezra 6).

At the halfway mark of the temple project, the prophet Zechariah received four more words (Zech. 7:1, 8:1, 9:1, 12:1). Three times within chapter seven, the prophet mentions, the "Word of the Lord that came to him" (Zech. 7:1, 4, 8). The term's first use is found in chapter four (Zech. 4:8), followed by chapter six (Zech. 6:8). Two more times, the term is used in chapter eight (Zech. 8:1, 18).

Note, the 'Word came' to the prophet; it was not conjured up, as with Judah's forefathers (Jer. 14:14). True prophecy 'Bubbles up (Heb. Naba), likened to flowing from a spontaneous fountain of life. The Hebrew word *Naba* is used for one speaking under the influence of the Holy Spirit to speak forth God's word. An example is seen in First Samuel, with king Saul, "When they came to Gibeah, behold, a group of prophets met him, and the Spirit of God rushed upon him, and he prophesied among them. And when all who knew him previously saw how he prophesied with the prophets, the people said to one another, 'What has come over the son of Kish? Is Saul also among the prophets'" (1 Sam. 10:10-11).

On the other hand, false prophecy is "Cooked" or "Boiled up" (Heb. Ziyd). The Hebrew word *Ziyd* can also be translated to act proudly, act presumptuously, act rebelliously, be presumptuous, be arrogant, and be rebelliously proud. An example of the Hebrew word *Ziyd* is found in Deuteronomy, "But the prophet who presumes to speak a word in my name that I have not commanded him to speak, or who speaks in the name of other gods, that same prophet shall die" (Deut. 18:20). Here, the false prophet had 'Presumed to speak on behalf of God, they had 'Cooked up' a false word to benefit themselves. Read Deuteronomy, chapter eighteen (vv. 15-22) for context.

As seen through the context of Deuteronomy (Deut. 18:15-22), when someone assumes to speak on behalf of God, and it does not come to pass, they are, by the biblical definition, a false prophet. Unfortunately, in recent times we have seen many from the Word of Faith and New Apostolic Reformation (NAR) movements prophecy falsely regarding COVID-19 and the re-election of President Trump. The 'prophets' arrogantly assumed to speak on God's behalf yet were evidently speaking from a proud heart. Essentially, they had 'Cooked up' a false word, and few have since repented. Under the Old Testament, the false prophet was to be stoned to death, while under the New Testament, the false prophet and teacher are to be sharply rebuked and avoided (Rom. 16:17, 1 Tim. 6:20, 2 Tim. 2:16, 3:5, Tit. 1:13).

Zechariah addressed Judah's false prophets in the opening chapter of this book, who God was, "Very angry with" (Zech. 1:2, cf. 7:12); they, "Did not listen" (Zech. 1:4, cf. 7:11-13) and subsequently perished (Zech. 1:5-6a, cf. 7:14). In chapter ten, the prophet Zechariah narrows in on them again (Zech. 10:2). God does not change (Num. 23:19, Heb. 13:8, Ja. 1:17). In the same way, God's people (Israel) were told to remove false prophets from their midst, Jesus told His followers to, "Watch out for false prophets" (Matt. 7:15-16). Paul says the same, warning that they will increase in the last days (1 Tim. 4:1-3), identifying them through their traits and teachings (1 Tim. 6:3-5). A false teacher and or false prophet are identified when their word does not come to pass when their teaching is unbiblical, and by the pursuit of their own interests, "Imagining that godliness is a means to gain" (1 Tim. 6:5). In sum, a false prophet and false teacher lead someone astray while seeking to benefit themselves, which was precisely the problem with Bethel, referenced in verse two (Zech. 7:2).

In the case of Zechariah, chapter seven, the word came in response to the people being sent from 'Bethel' (cf. Ezra 2:28) who sought the favour of the Lord (Zech. 7:2) inquiring about the fast days (Zech. 7:3) in remembrance of Jerusalem's destruction (2 Kgs. 25:8-10). Bethel is located twelve miles from Jerusalem, northwards, from where apostate worship had plagued the northern tribes of Israel (1 Kgs. 12:28-29, 13:1, Amos 7:13). First Kings is of particular interest where Jeroboam, "Said in his heart" (1 Kgs. 12:26) he would turn Israel away from God, turning them to other gods (1 Kgs. 12:28) and subsequently caused them to sin (1 Kgs. 12:30). The 'other gods' are the same Aaron made after leaving Egypt. "And he (Aaron) received the gold from their (Israel's) hand and fashioned it with a graving tool and made a golden calf. And they (Arron and company) said, 'These are your gods, O Israel, who brought you up out of the land of Egypt!'" (Exod. 32:4).

Jeroboam's actions polluted Israel for generations by introducing false gods ("Here are your gods") and sacrifices; his wickedness promoted the practice of false worship through idolatry, resulting in apostasy. When Arron did the same things, three-thousand lives were initially lost (killed) because of God's disapproval (Exod. 32:28). Following this, Moses announced that due to the great sin Israel had committed, he would seek forgiveness from God (Exod. 32:30-31). However, God responded, "Whoever has sinned against Me, I will blot out of My book" (Exod. 32:33).

The same threat of being, "Blotted out of the book of life" was given to the church of Sardis (Rev. 3:1-6), implying that the one who does not repent would have their name removed, as opposed to the one who does repent. The one who does repent, and remains in an overcoming state, would never have their name blotted out (Rev. 3:5). While some have never had their names written in the book of life (Rev. 13:8, 17:8, 20:12, 15), others have had them removed.

The church of Sardis was a Bethel type, promoting and practicing false worship, "Having a reputation of being alive, but was dead" (Rev. 3:1). The same was true of the false prophets and any other who deceived the people of God by introducing false worship. Aaron did it, Jeroboam did it, and those coming out of Bethel did it (Zech. 7:2) with their false feast and fasts (Zech. 7:5). The Bethelites were, in fact, on the same path as their ancestors (Zech. 7:8-13), with whom God had "Great anger" (Zech. 7:12).

The origin of Bethel's corruption is a result of Jeroboam's insecurity (1 Kgs. 12:26), who introduced false gods (1 Kgs, 12:28), false temples (1 Kgs. 12:31), false feast days (1 Kgs. 12:32-33), false sacrifices, and appointed false priests (1 Kgs. 12:31). Despite Jeroboam having great lineage and being appointed king by God (1 Kgs. 11:31, cf. 12:20, 14:7), he, "Did evil in the sight of God" (1 Kgs. 14:24). In response, God even sent a, "Man of God" (1 Kgs. 13:1) to publicly condemn Jeroboam's deception and false worship. The man of God predicted Bethel's future judgement where the false priest would be slaughtered (2 Kgs. 23:15-20). A sign confirming the word of Bethel's coming judgement was given through the man of God, with the tearing down of the alter (1 Kgs. 13:5). Jeroboam reacted to the prophecy negatively by attempting to lay a hand on the prophet, resulting in his hand drying up (1 Kgs. 13:4). The king then asked the prophet to, "Entreat favour of the Lord YOUR God" (not his God), asking him to pray for him (1 Kgs. 13:6). God did restore the king's hand - yet the shrivelling hand prophetically symbolised the king's authority, kingdom, life, and soul would likewise dry up. The evidence is further seen in the prophet's rejection of the king's hospitality, wanting nothing to do with him or anything he could offer (1 Kgs. 13:8-7-10), for it was condemned.

The prophet Amos confirms the prophecy of the, "Man of God" (1 Kgs. 13:1). Again, the warning given to the king was that it was not just him who would suffer God's judgment, but any following him (cf. 1 Kgs. 14:10-11). Because those following Jeroboam had departed from God's Law and its requirements, being the plumbline of righteousness (Isa. 28:17). The prophet Amos also confirms the demise of the king and his kingdom, including his temples at Bethel; all would crumble by the sword of God (Amos 7:9). Still, few listened. And like Jeremiah, the priest of Bethel conspired against the prophet, saying Amos was conspiring against the king (Amos 7:10), forbidding him from prophesying again in Bethel (Amos 7:13). Amos responds, "Now, therefore, hear the word of the LORD. 'You say, Do not prophesy against Israel, and do not preach against the house of Isaac.' Therefore, thus says the LORD: 'Your wife shall be a prostitute in the city, and your sons and your daughters shall fall by the sword, and your land shall be divided up with a measuring line; you yourself shall die in an unclean land, and Israel shall surely go into exile away from its land'" (Amos 7:16b-17).

Although Bethel (meaning 'House of God') is the place named by Jacob after God spoke to him (Gen. 35:15), as seen through the above-mentioned, it had become a place of corruption. Like the temple, which was purposed to be the 'Dwelling place of God', it was polluted and had polluted the whole land (Zech. 5). During the tribulation, the entire earth will be contaminated by the Babylonian system (the new world order, cf. Rev. 17-18), which is connected to the third temple (Zech. 5:11, cf. 2 Thess. 2:4).

Again, Zechariah, chapter seven, opened with the introduction of the men from Bethel (Zech. 1:2), who inquired of God through Zechariah (Zech. 7:3). God, through Zechariah, does not answer the Bethelites until the next chapter (Zech. 8:18-19). For the remainder of chapter seven, he instead reminds them of their forefathers (Zech. 7:7, cf. 1:2, 4-6a) who practiced empty rituals, that God hated (e.g., Isa. 1:11–17; Hos. 6:6; Amos 5:21–24). The same was true of the Bethelites, evident through their inquiry, indicating their feasting and fasting were for themselves and not for God (Zech. 7:5). Essentially, their empty hearts produced empty religious rituals, amounting to false worship.

In response to the Bethelites, the prophet's first word challenged their motivation (Zech. 7:4-7). The next word came (Zech. 7:8-10), warning and reminding the Bethelites of their forefathers; Do not be like them (cf. Zech. 8:16-17). Instead, "Render true judgements, show kindness, and mercy to one another" (Zech. 7:9). Judah's apostate ancestors (Jer. 5:6b) knew nothing of kindness and mercy; instead, they, "Oppressed the widow and fatherless and the sojourner" (Zech. 7:10) for their own greedy gain (Jer. 5:28). Instead of warning against evil and turning the people back to

God (Jer. 23:22), the prophets prophesied falsely, and the corrupt people loved it so (Jer. 5:11, cf. 2 Tim. 4:3). The false prophets said judgement would not come (Jer. 5:12), yet God said it would (Jer. 5:15-18), and when it did, the pre-emptive question was raised, "What will you do?" (Jer. 5:31).

"What will you do?" When the judgement of God came (Lam. 2:16-17), due to following the false and misleading apostate prophets (Lam. 2:14), the blind, and deaf people did not fear God (Jer. 5:21-22) and suffered unescapable bitter tribulation (Lam. 3:4-17). It was only then that they cried out to the Lord, "Remember me" (Lam 5:1), "Restore us" (Lam. 5:21), albeit too little, too late (Lam. 5:22).

So dire was the situation on that day that not one man cared about justice and sought truth (Zech. 7:9) - although God did look for one that would (Jer. 5:1). Moreover, none repented when challenged by God through the prophet Jeremiah (Jer. 5:3b, cf. 2:20). So rebellious was the previous generation; they "Refused to pay attention and turned a stubborn shoulder and stopped their ears that they might not hear" (Zech. 7:11), resulting in judgement (Zech. 7:14).

As seen in the earlier chapters, what God did to Judah's forefathers through His "Servant, Nebuchadnezzar" (Jer. 27:6, 43:10), He will do again during the tribulation through the antichrist. During the tribulation, the armies of the antichrist will scatter Judah, Israel, and Jerusalem" (Zech. 1:19, cf. Jer. 30:7, Dan 12:1) due to their apostasy. During the time of trouble, God's people will again do what they did when scattered previously (Zech. 7:14). They will cry out to God and repent of their sins (Lam. 5:16), hoping God will forgive them (Lam. 3:18-33). As seen through the writings of Jeremiah, when judged by God through Nebuchadnezzar, Judah's hope, in the end, was somewhat hopeless (Lam. 5:21b). The Jews had been dispersed, and their land was desolated (Zech. 7:14).

In sum, the introduction of men from Bethel (Zech. 7:2) gives cause for consideration and examination. Bethel was a corrupted place, polluting Israel for generations. Also mentioned above is the church of Sardis, which is a 'Bethel type', "Having a reputation of being alive, but was dead" (Rev. 3:2), albeit very dangerous! Today, there are many 'Bethel type' churches and movements that should be avoided. Numerous ones promote and worship "Another Jesus" through a "Different spirit and a different gospel" (2 Cor. 11:4). Fulfilling Paul's prophesies Bethel-type churches teach doctrines of demons and are increasing in these last days (1 Tim. 4:1, 2 Tim. 3:1, 4:3). In the same way, Jeroboam's insecurity (1 Kgs. 12:26) caused him and Judah to sin (1 Kgs. 12:30), many churches today do the same, corrupting God's word to attract and retain 'worshippers.' Following the example of the "Man of God," followers of Jesus Christ should have nothing to do with churches promoting and practicing false worship or be willing to receive anything from them, including their hospitality and or gifts. Any encountering a Bethel-type church should immediately leave and go another way (1 Kgs. 13:8-10).

CHAPER EIGHT

LASTING PEACE AND PROSPERITY

Jesus, Dwelling with His People
(Zech. 8:1-23)

To recap, Zechariah, chapter seven addressed false worship, narrowing in on those sent from Bethel (Zech. 7:2). Bethel was a place of corruption due to the requirements of worship having been tampered with (1 Kgs. 12). Defiled and false worship eventually resulted in tribulation (Lam. 3:5) - and will do again (Rev. 2:22) for the same reason.

The introduction for chapter eight, once again, is that the prophet received a word (Zech. 8:1). The word was, "I (God) am jealous for Zion, with great jealousy, and I am jealous for her with great wrath" (Zech. 8:2). Remember in chapter one where God was very angry with Judah's ancestors (Zech. 1:2, 7:11-14, 8:14) for not obeying Him, and yet He was exceedingly jealous over Jerusalem (Zech. 1:14). God is also exceedingly angry with the nations (Zech. 1:15) for troubling Israel. Now, as seen in this chapter and those following, God is turning things around, giving His people double for the trouble (Zech. 8:12-13, 9:12).

Especially during the tribulation, God becomes exceedingly jealous for Zion and exceedingly angry with the nations (cf. Joel 2:18). Following that time, God turns everything around where Jerusalem will finally be safe (Zech. 8:4-5). When Jerusalem is secure, it will be "Marvellous" (Zech. 8:6) for those seeing and experiencing it, mainly because it happens after the tribulation where Israel will face her greatest time of trouble in all history (Matt. 24:15-21, cf. Jer. 30:7, Dan. 12:1).

Leading up to the tribulation, God is regathering His people back into the land in fulfilment of prophecy. Keren Hayesod (meaning: Foundation fund) is a Jewish organisation raising funds and campaigning for Jews to migrate back to Israel. The campaign is called "Aliyah" (cf. Isa. 49:22). Aliyah means, 'The act of going up'. Today, the Jews are returning to the land, only to be scattered again during the time of trouble (Zech. 1:19-21, Dan. 12, Rev. 12).

Similarly, after the tribulation, God will gather Israel once more (Zech. 8:7-8) with a mere whistle (Zech. 10:8-12). Then, they will truly be His people after having been tried and tested through fire (Zech. 13:9). Once more, before peace and prosperity, tribulation must come, where God will set every man against his neighbour, once more (Zech. 8:11). The regathering of the Jews is one of the most significant end-time signs pointing towards Jesus' imminent return.

Following chapter seven, chapter eight contains the response (Zech. 8:19) to the question (Zech. 7:3) raised by the men from Bethel (Zech. 7:2) regarding the fast days (Zech. 7:3). The Bethelites inquired about the fast days that were in remembrance of Jerusalem's destruction, now being delivered from captivity after seventy years (Zech. 7:5). They wanted to know whether the fast days were still required. The answer (Zech. 8:19) comes through a second word (Zech. 8:18) of chapter eight, stating the fast would remain until and throughout the time of peace. The fast days are still practiced by Jews today, serving two purposes, 1). To remember what God did to Israel/Judah's ancestors, and 2). To look to what God will do in the future. In the future, instead of fasts in remembrance of past devastation, there will be feasts to celebrate peace and prosperity. The feasts will occur after Jesus returns and establishes His Messianic kingdom. Then there will be lasting peace because there is established truth (Zech. 8:19), silencing all flesh (Zech. 2:13). The established truth will not just be known to the Jews but to all nations (Zech. 8:.20-23, cf. 2:11). During the millennium, all nations will know and worship Jesus (Zech. 14:16–19, Isa. 2:3).

The fasts and feasts serve the same purpose as communion does today. Jesus committed this ordinance to the church to be followed as a continual reminder of His saving work through the cross. Communion must be commemorated until Christ returns (1 Cor. 11:23–26). The Lord's Supper reminds us of what took place through the cross and what will take place in the future, looking ahead to Christ's return. In the same way, as the Jews practice the fasts and feasts, Christians are to observe this supper until Jesus comes, "For as often as you eat this bread and drink this cup, you proclaim the Lord's death till He comes" (1 Cor. 11:26).

Like the communion ritual, chapter eight of the book of Zechariah now looks beyond the current time and the tribulation, into the millennial reign, where all the promises of God are fully realised. Chapter eight purposely follows a reminder to repent and return (Zech. 1:3) and to break away from empty religious rituals that serve man (Zech. 7:5-7, 8:14-17). Failing to do so would result in a repeat of God no longer hearing their prayers (Zech. 7:13a. cf. Jer. 11:10-11, Lam. 3:7-8, 5:22) and will no longer be with them ("Return to Me and [then] I will return to you"). Judah stopped listening to God (Zech. 7:11), so God stopped listening to them. In fact, for any who turns away from God's Law, even their prayers are an abomination (Prov. 28:9). Contrary to popular belief, God does not hear a sinner's prayer outside of repentance. Due to Judah's rebellion, as with any other in rebellion, God was no longer with their forefathers and therefore scattered them (Zech. 7:14).

As mentioned earlier, God will scatter Israel again during the tribulation (Zech. 1:19-21) for the same reasons He did previously. Judah ignored the warning, which was recorded in the first chapter, "Do not be like your fathers" (Zech. 1:4). Although they were once in covenant with God, they failed to return to Him (Zech. 1:3) by turning from their evil deeds (Zech. 1:4). The rebellious forefathers greatly angered God (Zech. 1:2, 7:12).

Chapter ten expands further on the problem stating Israel's religious leaders failed to shepherd the sheep (Zech. 10:3). As a result, the congregation (sheep) are now following false gods, believing utter nonsense, and being deceived by diviners' lies and false dreams (Zech. 10:2). Consequently, they are wandering like lost sheep without a shepherd.

In the previous section, Zechariah, chapter seven, titled "Beware of Bethel," king Jeroboam was identified as the one who set his heart on corrupting God's required worship to secure his kingdom. Despite Israel being warned not to worship God as the nations worship their gods (Deut. 12:4), they did whatever suited them (Deut. 12:8). Israel went wholly away from God because they failed to obey and practice His requirements by removing those who strayed (Deut. 12:32-13:1-5). The ones who strayed went as far as to promote, "Other gods" (Deut. 13:2). Jeroboam did the same things (1 Kgs. 12:28). Many 'Bethelite' seeker-sensitive churches do the same today to attract and retain members, especially those who regularly give. The "Other god" (Deut. 13:2) promoted in the corrupt churches today is "Another Jesus, presented through a, "Different spirit and gospel" (2 Cor. 11:4), hence the warning, "Beware of Bethel." The matter addressed in Zechariah, chapters seven (Zech. 7:9) and eight (Zech. 8:16, 19), is loving what God loves and hating what God hates. God hates false worship.

The problematic churches today are no different from Israel's ancestors, presenting a false god through a false gospel, offering false peace and prosperity (Jer. 6:14, 8:11, 28:9, cf. 1 Thess. 5:3). Peace and prosperity can only follow Christ's return (Zech. 8:3, Jer. 33). Until Jesus returns, anyone who claims peace and prosperity here and now is deceitful. As mentioned above, on and not before the return of Jesus, the faithless nation of Judah/Israel, who did not repent and turn from their evil deeds, only then will inherit the promise to, "Bring good to Jerusalem" (Zech. 8:15). After the time of trouble, the God, who is/was no longer with Israel because they were not with Him (Zech. 1:3), will return to them (Zech. 8:3, 8, 9:16) because they returned to Him (Zech. 10:9). God returning to His people is also promised in chapter two (Zech. 2:12).

When Jesus is dwelling with His people and ruling from Jerusalem (Zech. 10:6), He will then replace the faithless shepherds (Zech. 10:2), including those in the church. Truth (Zech. 8:16) will then be established instead of lies (Zech. 5:3) and holiness (Zech. 8:21) instead of evil deeds (Zech. 1:4). A desire to seek God, and His favour (Zech. 8:21-23) will replace a desire to satisfy self and obtain man's support and approval. Again, in those days, Jerusalem will be safe and secure for the first time outside of Solomon's rule (Zech. 8:4-6). Safe from outsiders, and insiders, such as the corrupt religious leaders.

Again, the only reason Jerusalem is safe and secure is that Jesus is ruling and reigning. Therefore, the big idea of Zechariah, chapter eight, is the return of Jesus, and the end of the age (Matt. 24:30), after the tribulation (Zech. 8:10). Such as a promise even for Zechariah's audience in 515 B.C., was, "Marvellous in their sight" (Zech. 8:6a) and, "Marvellous in God's sight" (Zech. 8:6b). In other words, it was unbelievable due to the impossibility. In response, God encouraged them, "Be strong" (Zech. 8:9) and,

"Fear not" (Zech. 8:13). What God said He would do, He will; despite the impossibility, God will save His people (Zech. 8:7).

The prophet's words were just as valid for his original audience (Zech. 8:9) as they are for us. At the time of Zechariah's writing, the Jews had returned from exile and were rebuilding the temple. The book of Zechariah revolves around the temple rebuild (Zech. 4:6-10, 6:11-14, 8:9-10), referring to the second temple, third, and fourth. The prophet Haggai presents the same message, stating the latter glory will be greater than the former (Hag. 2:9), referring to the millennial temple. If believing God's promise was difficult while rebuilding the second temple, how much more impossible would the promise be during the coming tribulation when the third temple is constructed? And then, while suffering the tribulation, to believe God will turn it around! (Zech. 8:14-15). Yet, God is faithful and able to do what He said He would do! Following the time of trouble, the millennial dispensation will see the fulfilment of the promise and serve as the actual 'reverse of the curse' (Deut. 28:37, Zech. 8:22-23), fully restoring and grafting Israel back in as Paul predicted (Rom. 9-11).

The book of Zechariah, thereby, should serve to ensure the reader God's promises are true and absolute. This is by pointing out, in the same way, He poured out judgement (Zech. 8:14-15, 7:11-14) and will again (Rev. 6-19), He will also deliver and save (Zech. 8:7). Through tribulation (Zech. 8:14), God has purposed to do good (Zech. 8:15). During the tribulation, God will save a remnant (Zech. 8:7, 12) who genuinely seek His face (Zech. 8:21) and follow Him wherever He goes (Rev. 14:4), even through fire (Zech. 13:9). The remnant will be set on doing the things God loves while avoiding the things He hates (Zech. 8:16-19).

In conclusion, Zechariah, chapter eight, proclaims that true and lasting peace and prosperity will only and always follow true and lasting repentance where true worship replaces false religion. True worship includes loving what God loves and hating what God hates. By failing these requirements, lasting peace cannot come before the time of trouble, purposed to prepare God's people for Christ's return. Jesus will return after the tribulation, responding to the Jews who call on His name (Matt. 23:39).

When Jesus returns, He will deal with the nations that troubled Israel (Zech. 1:21). Then He will set up His millennial kingdom and establish His rule and reign in the replacement of man ruling and reigning. Jesus will be the Shepherd, replacing Israel's worthless shepherds (Zech. 11:17). The same applies to the hirelings in the church today, such as the Laodicean type. Remember, Laodicea (Rev. 3:14-22) means 'People ruling'. The call for all generations is to return, repent and renew our covenant with God. Forsake false worship, and in doing so, revival will result, albeit due to most refusing to hear and respond now, revival will come through tribulation (Zech. 8:10, cf. Rev. 7:9), which is purposed to save (Zech. 8:8, 15, 10:6, 13:9).

CHAPTER NINE

BEHOLD, YOUR KING IS COMING TO YOU

'Ruined, Returned and Restored'
(Zech. 9:1-17)

Chapter nine starts with an introduction of "The burden of the Word of the Lord" (Zech. 9:1). It should be compared to Jeremiah's prophecy (Jer. 23:36, 38), where the false prophets opposed the, "Word of the Lord" (Jer. 6:13–14; 8:10–11; 14:14–16; 28:1–4, 10–11; 29:8–9, 20–23, 31–32) countering it with another, boiled up prophecy. Jeremiah's entire ministry was confronting and countering the pseudo prophets who were 'The burden' (Jer. 23:33) and were subsequently warned not to prophesy anymore. If they ignored the warning, the consequence was eternal judgement, stating, "I (God) will bring upon you (false prophet) everlasting reproach and perpetual shame, which shall not be forgotten" (Jer. 23:40).

In the case of Zechariah's words, like Jeremiah's, they presented both a threat (Zech. 9:1-8, cf. 12:1-6, 9) and a blessing (cf. Zech. 9:9-17, cf. 12:7-8), yet, either-or, the message is directed towards, and purposed for salvation. For example, verses nine and seventeen in chapter nine (Zech. 9:9, 11-17) describe the blessing for those awaiting the Messiah. In contrast, verses one to eight, ten, and thirteen (Zech. 9:1-8, 10a, 13) warn of judgement for those rejecting Him. Still, alternately pointing toward peace (Zech. 9:10b) for those inheriting salvation (Zech. 9:9b, 16, cf. Isa. 11:6-9).

Like Isaiah, Zechariah's prophecy is in two parts: the prophetic promise of the Messiah's first appearing (Zech. 9:9, cf. Matt. 21:12), and the second where He will judge the nations (Zech. 9:10). The two separate appearances are divided by the church age as also described by Isaiah (Isa. 9:6–7; 61:1–2; cf. Lk. 4:18–21), albeit was not revealed until after Jesus had been resurrected. Jesus' first appearance was to take away the sins of the world (Zech. 12:10, cf. Jn. 1:29); His mission was to seek and save the lost (Lk. 19:10). His next appearance will be to deliver those seeking His face (Zech. 9:9-17, 12:12-13:1) and to judge sinners rejecting Him and His sacrifice for sin (Zech. 9:1-8, 10a, 13).

Most conservative scholars regard the first section of Zechariah, chapter nine (Zech. 9:9:1–8) as a fulfilled prophecy of the conquests of Alexander the Great throughout the area of Palestine. Zechariah, living in the days of the Medo-Persian Empire, predicted the coming Grecian Empire (Zech. 9:1–8, 13), the Roman Empire (Zech. 11:4–14), and Israel's future in the last days (chaps. 12–14). However, as stated beforehand, the prophecy bypasses the events of the Persians, the Greeks, and the Romans, pointing towards the return of Jesus Christ.

As mentioned elsewhere, leading up to the second coming, war is one of the most significant end times signs (Matt. 24:6, Rev. 6:4), where the nations will rally against Israel (Zech. 11:8-20, 12:3) and God will respond (Zech. 1:21, 12:9). The words, "For the LORD has an eye on mankind, and all the tribes of Israel" (Zech. 9:1) confirm that God is watching closely and indicates He will judge. And although the nations think, "They are very wise" (Zech. 9:2b), who are at rest (Zech. 1:11), and at ease (Zech. 1:15), God is, "Exceedingly angry with them" (Zech. 1:15) for troubling Israel. When God repays the 'Very wise' (Zech. 9:2) nations for their treatment of Israel, they will be afraid (Zech. 9:5a), and they shall, "Writhe in anguish because their hopes are confounded" (Zech. 9:5b).

Within the prophecy, included with the 'Very wise' (Zech. 9:2) nations troubling Israel is Damascus (Zech. 9:1), one of Israel's greatest enemies. Damascus joins the nation who is at ease and is of particular interest due to the unfulfilled prophecy in Isaiah (Isa. 17). Isaiah predicts Damascus will, "Cease to be a city and will become a heap of ruins" (Isa. 17:1). Arguably, Damascus will be struck by Israel just before or early after the tribulation has commenced. During "The hour of trial" (Rev. 3:10), "The nations roar like the roaring of many waters, but He (God) will rebuke them, and they will flee far away chased like chaff" (Isa. 17:13, Zech. 9:5). The roaring nations would include Russia, which is Syria's ally.

God destroys Russia when they too attack Israel (Ezek. 38-39, Dan. 11:40-45). Other nations possibly responding when Israel destroys Damascus are those mentioned in Psalm eighty-three (Ps. 83), identified as a ten-nation confederation. They too assume they can possess Israel (Ps. 83:12). Despite the supposed wisdom of the nations, God will effortlessly deal with them, "At evening time, behold terror, before morning, they are no more" (Isa. 17:14, cf. Ps. 83:13-18, cf. Zech. 9:5). Due to sheer devastation, the destruction of Damascus could be the event that activates the Middle East Peace Treaty (cf. Isa. 28:15, 18, Dan. 9:24-27) triggering the tribulation. Again, Alexandra did not fulfil this prophecy; therefore, it remains to be fulfilled and will be fulfilled during the coming tribulation, evident in verse ten (Zech. 9:10).

Alongside Damascus, Tyre and Sidon are also of particular interest, addressed by God through the prophet Joel, "What are you to me, O Tyre and Sidon, and all the regions of Philistia? Are you paying Me back for something? If you are paying Me back, I will return your payment on your own head swiftly and speedily" (Joel 3:4). Tyre and Sidon are the Phoenicians (Lebanon) and the Philistines (Palestinians) who took advantage economically of Judah's demise (cf. Ezek. 25:15; 28:20–24), and while they experienced the judgement of God through King Nebuchadnezzar, Alexander the Great, and Artaxerxes. However, Joel's prophecy is still to be fulfilled. Joel is also joined by Isaiah (Isa 23), Jeremiah (Jer. 25, 27, 47), Ezekiel (Ezek. 26-28), and Amos (Amos 1:9-10). Zechariah's prophecy (Zech. 9:1-4) fits within the same timeline.

Tyre and Sidon are also mentioned in the New Testament, in the company of Sodom, being a region Jesus spent time in (Mk. 7:21) and did miracles (Mk. 7:31), ministering to great multitudes (Lk. 6:17). When addressing Chorazin and Bethsaida (Lk. 10:13), Jesus refers to Tyre and Sidon's judgement, stating Chorazin and Bethsaida's judgement would be worse due to what they had been given. Although Tyre and Sidon had an opportunity to repent and did not, they will be treated lightly by comparison to those hearing the gospel and witnessing miracles, "That servant who knows his master's will but does not get ready or follow his instructions will be beaten with many blows. But the one who unknowingly does things worthy of punishment will be beaten with few blows. From everyone who has been given much, much will be required; and from him who has been entrusted with much, even more, will be demanded" (Lk. 12:47-48).

Again, following the tribulation when Jesus returns, "On a day when nobody expects" (Lk. 12:46), after the judgement, universal peace will be eternally established (Zech. 9:10b). God's oppressed and imprisoned people will be delivered and restored, double for the trouble (Zech. 9:11-12).

Again, Israel has never experienced peace since the rule of King Solomon. From that time until this day, there has been an ongoing conflict between the Jews and pretty much everyone else. Yet, when Jesus returns (Zech. 9:9b, 14, 16), He will protect, save (Zech. 9:15, 16), and prosper them (Zech. 9:12, 17). Again, the prophecy will be fulfilled after the tribulation period, evident by the words, "Behold, your King is coming to you" (Zech. 9:9).

The prophecy of the coming King was partly fulfilled with Jesus' first appearance (cf. Matt. 21:1-5) and will be fulfilled with His next. On His next appearing (Matt. 24:30), Israel will inherit salvation (Zech. 9:9a, 16, cf. Isa. 62:11) and be restored (Zech. 9:12, 17). The symbolism of Jesus, "Mounted on a donkey" (Zech. 9:9) implies peace, not prosperity, as the charismatic's (Word of Faith) falsely claim. Zechariah's audience knew that if a king came on a donkey, it meant he came in peace, yet if he came on a stallion, it meant war. The next time Jesus appears, He will be riding a white horse (stallion), indicating war, and the Revelation prophecy confirms it, Jesus will wage war against His enemies (Rev. 19:11-15). After the war, Jesus will then establish true and lasting peace (Zech. 9:10b).

When Jesus returns, judges the nations, and establishes peace (Zech. 9-10-10:12), He will also deal with the worthless shepherds (Zech. 11:17), against whom His anger is hot (Zech. 10:3). Those remaining faithful to His covenant will likewise experience His covenant faithfulness (Zech. 9:11), returning and restoring them - His people (Zech. 9:12). At the end of the tribulation, God will gather Israel, once again, with a mere 'Whistle' (Zech. 10:8). Israel's hope (Zech. 9:12) rests entirely on this Messianic promise. God will return and restore the Jews.

Although The Jews have been returned to the Land of Israel (1948), the prophecy is partly fulfilled. As mentioned earlier, the Jews are still yet to be re-scattered and will be again during the tribulation (Zech. 1:19-21,

Dan. 12, Matt. 24:15, Rev. 12). In the same way, Judah had hope during the exile tribulation (Lam. 3:5); as prisoners of hope (Zech. 9:12, Lam. 3:21-33), they will again during the great tribulation, causing them to call on Jesus' name, triggering His return (Matt. 23:39). During the tribulation, the Jews will also fight back against the nations persecuting them (Zech. 9:13, 12:3). Israel fighting back against her oppressors is a repeat of what took place through the Maccabees when Antiochus, the 'Son of Greece' (Zech. 9:13) who established himself in the temple (cf. Dan. 8:9-14, 11:32). Antiochus was an antichrist type, foreshadowing the antichrist to come (Matt. 24:15, 1 Thess. 2, Rev. 13). In the same way, God gave Israel victory over Antiochus, He will again over the antichrist, albeit, like last time, many will perish (Dan. 11:33); in fact, most will (Zech. 13:8-9). Still, victory is assured from God, who will, "Wield Israel, like a warrior's sword" (Zech. 9:13). Israel will be likened to God's 'Arrow' going, "Forth like lightening" (Zech. 9:14), putting their enemies to shame (Zech. 10:5). When God, "Sounds the trumpet," Israel will, "March forth in the whirlwinds of the south" (Zech. 9:14), under God's protection, devouring anything and everyone in their path (Zech. 9:15).

Previously, and again through the tribulation, God scatters Israel among the nations like a "Whirlwind" (Zech. 7:14, cf. 1:18-20). Towards the end of the time of trouble, God will be with Israel due to repentance through fire (Zech.13:9). And if God is for them, who can be against them? (Rom. 8:31), which is why they are encouraged to, "Be strong" (Zech. 8:9, 13) and, "Fear not" (Zech. 8:13, 15). "On that day," at the sound of the trumpet (Zech. 9:14), God will deliver and save His people (Zech. 8:13, 9:16, 12:9).

The reference to the sounding trumpet (Zech. 9:14) is at the end of the tribulation. "On that day the Lord their God will save them" (Zech. 9:16), and anyone joining themselves to the Lord, through the Jews will also be saved (Zech. 2:11, 8:22). The words, "On that Day" refer to the establishment of the millennial kingdom, used eighteen times in the book of Zechariah. Chapter nine, verse sixteen (Zech. 9:16) first uses the term, seen again in chapter eleven (Zech. 11:11), six more times in chapter twelve (Zech. 12:3, 4, 6, 8, 9, 11), three times more in chapter thirteen (Zech. 13:1, 2, 4) and seven times in chapter fourteen (Zech. 14:4, 6, 8, 9, 13, 20, 21).

When Jesus returns, instead of Israel being an example of God's righteous judgement (Zech. 8:13), "On that Day" they will be an example of God's goodness (Zech. 9:17, cf. 8:14-15). Israel will, "Shine in the land" (Zech. 9:16). Instead of war - they will have peace (cf. Amos 9:11-15). That which the locust has eaten will be restored (Joel 2:21-27), double for the trouble (Zech. 9:12).

At this point, there should not be any need to reiterate the promise of receiving. Double for the trouble is directed at Israel, not the church or any other individual claiming it for themselves.

In conclusion, the 'Burden of the word of the Lord' refers to judgement and blessing, yet always pointing towards salvation. Salvation is on offer for the Jews (Zech. 1:3, 2:5, 10:6, 12:7-9, 13:1) and the Gentiles (Zech. 2:11, 8:20-23, 9:10, 14:16). The message to all is, "Return to Me, and I will [then] return to you" (Zech. 1:3, Joel 2:12, cf. Jas. 4:8). Those who do can expect peace and prosperity. Those who do not can expect to be terrified (Isa. 17:14, cf. Ps. 83:13-18, Zech. 9:5). As seen through chapter eight, without Christ, there can be no lasting peace and prosperity. Lasting peace and prosperity cannot and will not come before Jesus returns.

CHAPTER TEN

WITH A WHISTLE

'Remembered, Returned, Revived and Restored'
(Zech. 10:1-12)

The promised blessings of chapter nine continue in chapter ten. Also, as in chapter nine, before the announcement of the blessings comes the warning to Israel's enemies. Chapter nine talks about Israel's external enemies, while chapter ten addresses their internal enemies. God reminds both external and internal troublemakers that He is in absolute control over every matter.

Chapter ten clears up any confusion; God commands every matter, including the weather, by providing the rain (Zech. 10:1), producing the grain, and not, "The household gods that utter nonsense" (Zech. 10:2). A lesson further learned in the millennium, where rainfall is withheld from the rebels who fail to worship God (Zech. 14:18-19).

Everything good comes from God, especially salvation (Ja. 1:17-19). On the contrary, nothing good comes from the false shepherds, against whom God's "Anger is hot" (Zech. 10:3a.cf. 1:2). Nothing good comes from them, and nothing good will become of them. God will "Punish the leaders" (Zech. 10:3b) for their treachery. When Jesus returns, God will put an end to religious corruption, and He will deliver His people from the failing shepherds (cf. Mic. 5:4).

The issue of false worship was addressed in chapters seven and eight concerning the Bethelites and is now further discussed concerning the diviners telling lies through false dreams (like Bethelites today). Through deception and empty counsel (void of wisdom), the hirelings of chapter ten cause the sheep to stray (Zech. 10:2), resulting in Israel being scattered (Zech. 10:9, 2:18-21). The reason the dreamers have any influence in the first place is due to a lack of shepherds (Zech. 10:2). This is not to say there are no shepherds at all, but rather, no faithful shepherds, as Israel's religious leaders have neglected their duties and responsibilities before God and towards His people.

As mentioned in chapters eight and nine, many 'Bethelite' churches also practice false worship, telling lies, giving false words, and dreams. These diviners (Christian clairvoyants) will suffer the same treatment that Judah's ancestors did (Zech. 1:4-5), to be repeated in the future. Soon, Israel will re-experience God's judgement through the coming tribulation. Israel's leaders have been and are being warned through all the prophets in the same way the church has been. They are being warned through the written and spoken word, particularly through the seven letters to the seven churches (Rev. 2-3).

Besides Zechariah, another example of Israel being warned of the coming judgement is through the prophet Zephaniah; there, God again addressed Israel's shepherds. Through the prophet God calls them rebellious, complacent men (Zeph. 1:12, 3:1), fickle prophets, and profane priests (Zeph. 3:4) who refuse to listen and accept correction (Zeph. 3:2). The failing shepherds thought God was not bothered either way with what they did and said (Zeph. 1:12b). Some bowed down to God, and Milcom

WITH A WHISTLE

(Molech) (Zeph. 1:5), and others claimed to be God in denial of the living God (Zeph. 2:15b). Despite their belief, that God will not judge them, He has reserved a day (Zeph. 1:10, 3:11, 16) and a time (Zeph. 1:12, 3:9, 19, 20-x2) where He will judge them with burning anger, where all the earth shall be consumed (Zeph. 3:8c).

As with Zechariah, Zephaniah accompanying the threat, the invitation for salvation is announced: before all the judgement takes place, "Seek the Lord" (Zeph. 2:3a, Zech. 1:3). Because of the calamity coming upon the whole earth (Zeph. 2:2, cf. Rev. 3:10), God warns, "Be humble, do His just commands, seek righteousness, and seek humility" (Zech. 2:3b, Zech. 1:3, 8:8-10). In other words, "Love what God loves and hate what God hates" (Zech. 8:16-17); by doing so, they might avoid the coming judgement (Zeph. 2:3c).

Ezekiel likewise prophesied against the shepherds (Ezek. 34:1-10, cf. Zech. 1:2, 10:3), accusing them of feeding themselves (Ezek. 34:2, 8) at the expense of the sheep (Ezek. 34:3-6). Like with Zechariah, Through Ezekiel, God says, "Since there was no shepherd, His people are afflicted" (Ezek. 34:80, Zech. 10:2). Again, as through Zechariah, Ezekiel states God is against the shepherds (Ezek. 34:10, Zech. 10:3) and will rescue His people from them (Ezek. 34:11, Zech. 10:6). Ezekiel likewise states that when God rescues His people, He will bring them into their own land (Ezek. 34:13, Zech. 10:6, 10). Jesus will be the Shepherd (Ezek. 34:14) of the human sheep (Ezek. 34:31).

Through Ezekiel, like Zechariah, God scolds the worthless shepherds (Zech. 10:3, 11:17) who not only feed themselves at the expense of the sheep but make it so the sheep cannot feed at all (Ezek. 34:17-19). The false shepherds have failed to keep the sheep and keep the wolves at bay, what's worse, they have become the wolves (cf. Matt. 7:15). These self-serving hirelings, these, "Worthless shepherds, who dessert the flock" (Zech.

11:17), have thus forgotten who controls what (Zech. 10:1) and that God will judge them for failing to care for His people (Zech. 10:3), despite not believing that He will (Zeph. 1:12b). The same was true of Judah's forefathers; "Where are they now?" (Zech. 1:5-6).

As seen through Ezekiel (Ezek. 34) and Zechariah (Zech. 10), where Israel's leaders failed to fulfil their responsibilities (Zech. 10:3), God, however, succeeds (Zech. 10:3b-12). Again, when Jesus returns, He will deliver and save His people (Zech. 10:6a) and bring them back into the Land (Zech. 10:6b, 8, 9, 10). With a mere 'Whistle' He will do it (Zech. 10:8). Once more, God is in control; with a 'Whistle,' He can command the insects (Isa. 7:18) and His people (Jug. 5:16, Zech. 10:8) in the same way He controls the storm clouds that provide rain (Zech. 10:1).

God gives charge over everything, the weather (Zech. 10:1), the insects and the beasts of the field, the nations (Zech. 1:18-21), and His people (Zech. 10:8). In the end, God reverses everything; what will be destroyed is restored, and where Israel's land is devastated, God restores it and them with 'Latter rain' (Joel. 2:23).

Joel's reference to the 'Latter rain' (Joel 2:23) refers to this season of blessing. While Joels speaks of a natural season contextually, the reference is also allegoric, applying a blessing. Yet, the timing of the season is often misquoted alongside Haggai's reference to, "Latter glory" (Hag. 2:9). The latter glory points to the millennial temple. Both references point to Jesus, the 'Cornerstone' (Zech. 10:4); when He is ruling on the earth - He reverses the curse and pours out blessings on His people.

When Jesus returns, God will redeem His people (Zech. 10:8), and leading up to His return, God will make Israel strong (Zech. 10:5b, 12a). God will bring them back into remembrance of Him (Zech. 10:9), where they will walk with Him (Zech. 10:12b). Again, in doing so, God does the opposite of the shepherds, who made the people weak, wander, forget, and forsake God. In the same way, God causes the rain to fall and the plants to grow (Zech. 10:1), He will restore and replenish His people. He will also repay those who brought spiritual drought through false prophecy and false teaching, driven by wrong motives.

The means and method in which God brings the Jews back to Him (cf. Zech. 1:3) are by redirecting their focus on the coming King, the Messiah - this is seen in verse four (Zech. 10:4). The terms "Cornerstone" (cf. Isa. 28:16), the, "Tent Peg,"… the "Battle bow" (cf. Ps. 45:5), and the, "Ruler" (cf. Gen. 49:10; Micah 5:2) all point toward the strong, stable, reliable, and trustworthy nature and rule of Jesus.

As mentioned earlier, Bethel-type churches commit the same sins Israel's ancestors did, causing their followers to forget God. Followers of Bethel-type churches forget God due to being deceived and distracted and through a lack of fear. By redirecting Bethelites to the return of Jesus, the fear of God and holiness will return.

Joining Judah's ancestors (Zech. 1:5, Zeph. 1:12b), many today say God will not judge the church. However, the church was warned that if she did what Israel did, she would get the same treatment (Rom. 11:22). Most hyper-grace Bethel-type churches, like Israel, will not see and respond to the warning and message of the coming King until the tribulation commences.

"Until the fullness of the Gentiles has come in" (Rom. 11:25), Israel will not see (have knowledge of) their Messiah due to being temporarily blinded. The "Fullness of the Gentiles" refers to the church, which will be removed before the tribulation (Rev. 3:10). "At the sound of the trumpet of God," those looking for Jesus will be raptured (1 Thess. 4:16, cf. Lu. 21:34-36). Israel also had the opportunity, as seen through the prophet Zephaniah, "Perhaps you may be hidden on the day of the anger of the Lord" (Zeph. 2:3c), to escape the things to come. Yet, they failed and will therefore have another chance to get right with God during the time of trial. Those who do will be used mightily by God in evangelism and warfare.

As seen in Zechariah, chapter nine, God will wield Israel like a warrior's sword (Zech. 9:13), which is repeated in chapter ten; Israel will be like God's, "Majestic steed in battle" (Zech. 10:3). They, "Shall be like mighty men in battle, they all fight because the Lord is with them, and they shall put to shame the riders on the horses" (Zech. 10:5). Following a return to the Lord (Zech. 1:3, Joel 2:12, 13), in the tribulation, the weak among Israel will become warriors (Joel. 3:10).

Today, Zachariah's prophecy is being fulfilled where the Jews are returning to the Land (Zech. 10:9-10) in preparation for the coming tribulation, which the millennial dispensation will follow. During the tribulation, the Jews remember God (Zech. 10:9). They return to Him (Zech. 1:3) and put their trust in Him (Zech. 10:1). Instead of trusting in idols (Zech. 10:2) and false shepherds who led them astray, they call on Jesus' name, and God will answer them (Zech. 10:6, Matt. 23:39).

Despite some teaching replacement theology, God has not forgotten, forsaken, or replaced Israel with the church (Zech. 10:6), and neither will He overlook the deeds of the failing shepherds. The false shepherds today, for Israel, are those rejecting Jesus Christ as their Messiah and will direct the Jews to the antichrist instead.

Still, during the time of trouble, many Jews will recognise and reject the antichrist (Dan. 11:33, 12:10, Rev. 13:18); they will return to God by accepting Jesus Christ and walking with Him (Zech. 10:12, Rev. 14:4). At the commencement of the tribulation, the Jews will be sealed by the Spirit of Christ (Rev. 7:4). Then, through the Jews, God will bring about revival during, "The hour of trial that is coming on the whole world, to try those who dwell on the earth" (Rev. 3:10). The greatest revival in the history of man is reserved for the tribulation (Joel 2:28-32). What Peter experienced in Joel's prophecy foreshadowed the things to come (Acts 2:17-21, Matt. 24:29).

Again, as with the misquotation of Joel and Haggai, the 'Latter rain' (glory), many claim the coming tribulation revival for the church age. Pentecostals, in particular, believe there will be one last great revival before the church is raptured. Depending on what country they live in generally determines where that great revival will occur. For the British, it is the UK; for the Americans, the USA, and Australians, it is the land Down Under, the great south land of the Holy Spirit. There is no evidence of these claims that surpass scripture. However, the scripture's limited confirmation states that the church participated in the part-fulfillment of Joel's prophecy (Joel 2:28-23, Acts 2:17-21), and Israel will participate in the fulfilment of it (Matt. 24:14, 29, Rev. 7:9). In sum, the great revival to come will occur in the tribulation.

In the tribulation, not only will God revive the Jews, but people from every nation (Rev. 7:9-10, Zech. 2:11, 8:20-23, 14:16-21). In the closing seven years of this age, the gospel will be preached to every nation, primarily through the Jews (Rev. 7:4-9), fulfilling prophecy (Matt. 24:14) in preparation for Christ's return. In the same way, God turns everything around for Israel; He uses them, who rejected their Messiah, to proclaim Him. Again, during the tribulation, the Jews will lead countless millions to Christ (Rev. 7:9, Dan. 11:33).

In conclusion, with a mere whistle (Zech. 10:8), God will turn the apostate situation of the Jews (and the lukewarm church) around. Where there is no fear, faith, and faithfulness, God will create something out of nothing, such as the nation of Israel (Isa. 66:8, Ezek. 37:3). He will bring His people back (Zech. 10:9) into the Land (Zech. 10:8), even against any and every obstacle (Zech. 10:11). Soon, He will complete this promise as He did through Moses, removing every barrier. God, who once had rejected His people (Zech. 10:6), will again shortly redeem them (Zech. 10:8). In doing so, they shall remember Him (Zech. 10:9). They will be strengthened by Him, and they will walk with God (Zech. 10:12). God will also put an end to the false shepherds (Zech. 10:3) and any other resisting His rule (Zech. 10:5, 11b).

CHAPTER ELEVEN

DOOMED TO SLAUGHTER

'Woe to the Worthless Shepherd'
(Zech. 11:1-17)

Recapping chapters eight, nine, and ten reveals blessings and curses, blessings for the faithful and curses for the faithless and troublemakers. Chapters eight and nine aimed at the external enemies of Israel (Zech. 9:1-4), while chapter ten addressed internal enemies, the failing shepherds (Zech. 10:2-3). All passages are Messianic, pointing towards the return of Christ (Zech. 8:3, 8, 20-23, 9:9, 10:4, 12). Chapter eleven continues with the same theme of the Messiah returning, ruling, and reigning while continuing to aim at Israel's internal enemies, the "Foolish" and "Worthless shepherd" (Zech. 11:15, 17). In sum, the chapter reveals that when Jesus returns, He will judge His cursed enemies and bless His faithful followers. The enemies of God are defined by those rejecting His Son, Jesus, and turning others away from Him, the True Shepherd (Zech. 11:4-14).

The theme of chapter eleven is essentially Christ's return and God's pronounced judgement against Israel's faithless flock (Zech. 11:4) and her 'Foolish shepherds' (Zech. 11:15). It covers the entire land from north to south, indicated by the reference to Lebanon, Bashan, and Jordon (Zech. 11:1-3). When the judgement falls, Israel's shepherd will wail over her devastation (Zech. 11:3). In the same way the merchants will wail over the coming destruction of Babylon (Rev. 18), the coming new world order. On both counts, the destruction encourages the inhibiter to break away from the world and return to God (Zech. 1:3, Rev. 18:4), to separate themselves to God by coming out of Babylon and out of the Babylonian (new world) system.

As always, yet especially during the tribulation, there is a contrast between Jesus Christ and the antichrist, seemingly competing for worship. At the halfway point of the seven-year event (the tribulation), the angels proclaim the gospel, "Fear God and worship Him" (Rev. 14:7). It is competing with the false prophet deceiving with lying signs and wonders and directing the global population to worship the beast and take his mark (Rev. 13:11-18). Zechariah, chapter eleven reveals the same, contrasting the Messiah against the 'Foolish' (Zech. 11:15) and 'Worthless shepherd' (Zech. 11:17). The foolish and worthless shepherd is ultimately the antichrist (Zech. 11:4-14) but includes any failing shepherds whom God's anger is hot against (Zech. 10:3). The faithless shepherd's condition and preparing the flock for the antichrist, and when the time comes, they will hand-deliver them over to him. Instead of leading the people of God to repentance, they caused them to, "Wander like sheep" (Zech. 10:2), wandering into the path of destruction (Zech. 11:4, 7).

Remembering the first chapter again, with the announcement, "Return to Me and [then] I will return to you" (Zech. 1:3), which is a call to repent and rebuild. Also, in the previous chapter (Zech. 10), where God says He will deal with the 'Shepherds' (Zech. 10:3) who have caused the sheep to wander (Zech. 10:2-3). Chapter eleven builds on the threat and announcement of pending judgement because Israel's leaders failed to meet and direct the sheep to walk in the ways of God.

Although Zechariah's audience said they would repent (Zech. 1:6a), the reality was that they did not, and have not until this day, which is why they were, and are, "Doomed for slaughter" (Zech. 11:4). As mentioned above, Israel is especially doomed for slaughter due to following the self-indulgent shepherds, who will ultimately cause them to follow the 'Foolish shepherd' (Zech. 11:15) to come.

Not only do Israel's leaders (Zech. 10:3) fail to direct the flock in the ways of God, they used them for greedy gain. The failing shepherds (Zech. 10:3), "Bought and sold" (Zech. 11:5) and "Traded" (Zech. 11:7, 11) the flock, saying, "Blessed be the Lord, I have become rich" (Zech. 11:5). The shepherds traded the flock to be devoured (Zech. 11:16), doomed for slaughter, for personal profit (Zech. 11:7). At this point, neither the failing shepherds nor God pities the flock predestined for destruction (Zech. 11:6). On the day of judgement, God will not pity the failing shepherd nor the faithless sheep who followed them (cf. Jer. 13:12-14). However, He will pity the faithful remnant who are also, "Doomed to be slaughtered by the sheep traders" (Zech. 11:7).

Going further in their refusal to follow God and lead the flock in the ways of God, they detested Him, the True Shepherd (Zech. 11:8). This resulted in their fate being sealed, where the covenant was revoked (Zech. 11:9-11). The rejection of Jesus was subsequent in the spiritual blinding of Israel (Rom. 11:25). Again, the failing shepherds bought, sold (Zech. 11:5), and traded the flock (Zech. 11:7) so that they would become rich (Zech. 11:5) and did likewise with Jesus, as prophesied. For, "Thirty pieces of silver" (Zech. 11:13). The amount thirty pieces of silver is an insult; instead of paying the wages due, a smaller sum was drawn and tossed into the field (Zech. 11:12-13).

Clearly, the prophecy was fulfilled by Judas, who rejected Jesus for thirty pieces of silver. He then tossed the money at the feet of the religious leaders, who then purchased the potter's field with the money (Matt. 26:14-16, 27:3-10). For both Judas and Israel, for this act, their union (communion—common-union) with God was broken (Zech. 11:14). Where there was once grace and favor, there is now disfavor and disgrace. The breaking of the staff signified the breaking of the covenant, and those watching knew at once that the word of the Lord had been spoken (Zech. 11:11). Essentially, Israel is no longer in covenant with God due to the rejection of Jesus.

Essentially, Zechariah is predicting that what happened in the past will occur again. The prophet Jeremiah addressed the same issue of the greedy shepherds (Jer. 22:13-17), who scatter the sheep (Jer. 23:1-3), to be later regathered by Jesus (Jer. 23:3-8). Like Zechariah (Zech. 10:2-3), Jeremiah also narrows in on the false message of the prophets leading Judah astray (Jer. 23:16-17), pronouncing judgement in the latter days (Jer. 23:18-22). When judgement falls, a remnant will wake from their spiritual slumber.

The faithful remnant is those turning to Christ during the tribulation and then slaughtered (Rev. 6:9-11, 12:11). While the passage is prophetic, pointing to the rejection of the Messiah (Zech. 11:8-13), it also includes others who have been slaughtered for following Jesus, starting with His disciples. When the Shepherd (Jesus) was struck, the sheep (disciples) were scattered, cut off, and slaughtered (Zech. 13:7-9). Many faithful followers of Christ perished during the first centuries, and many more have since, yet most will die during the tribulation (Zech. 13:9).

As mentioned above, during the tribulation, God will pity a remnant within Israel (Zech. 8:6, 11, 12, 9:7). He will favor them, bringing them back into union throughout and after the seven-year event (Zech. 11:7). By doing so, "In one month," God first destroys and replaces the "Three shepherds" whom He became "Impatient" with, who "Detested" Him (Zech. 11:8). God will destroy Israel's failing leaders before He deals with the antichrist (Zech. 11:17). The three shepherds represent Israel's leaders, whom God will punish (Zech. 10:3), probably consisting of kings (government officials), priests, and prophets. God holds these failing shepherds responsible for causing the sheep to wander (Zech. 10:2). Yet, there is also still individual accountability (Zech. 12:12-14, cf. Isa. 45:23, Rom. 14:12).

Since Israel has still not answered the call and met the requirement of accepting and submitting to their Messiah, they have not been cleansed (Zech. 13:1). Therefore, the threat of judgement, the worst to come (Jer. 30:7, Dan. 12:1, Matt. 24:21), is still yet to be realised.

The prophecy will be achieved in two parts. The first part was performed in 70 A.D. with the fall of Jerusalem (Zech. 11:8-14), following Judas' betrayal of Jesus, in fulfilment of prophecy (Zech. 11:12-13). Because Israel rejected the Messiah, they fell into their neighbours' hands and the King, who crushed the land (Zech. 11:6), causing them to flee and be scattered (Zech. 10:9). Again, the future and final judgement is still ahead of Israel—and also us, as prescribed due to the 'Worthless shepherd' (Zech. 11:17) seeking to rule in replacement of God is yet to come. As mentioned earlier, the worthless shepherd is the one rejecting Jesus Christ (1 Jn. 4:1-6) and claiming to be the Messiah (2 Thess. 2:4). He will also be the one attempting to block the prophetic fulfilment of Jesus' second coming as the returning and ruling King by killing Jews.

Israel rejected the True Shepherd at His first appearance, and they will reject Him before His second appearance by accepting the 'Worthless shepherd' (Zech. 11:17), the antichrist. The antichrist will soon appear, claiming rule over the Jewish people. However, like the failing shepherds, the antichrist will not have any concern for their welfare or pity them as they perish (Zech. 11:16) by his hand (Zech. 11:16). Like the shepherds before him, he will only care about his own interests. However, when Jesus returns, the antichrist's strength (right arm) and intelligence (eye) will be destroyed (Zech. 11:17). He who destined the sheep for slaughter will be slaughtered.

In sum, before the antichrist is judged, during the coming tribulation, he will take up his place in the third temple, ruling from Jerusalem (2 Thess. 2:4). From there, he will be set on destroying the Jews (Dan. 11:41, Rev. 12:13) and the left behind, saints (Rev. 13:7). The act is arguably designed to block Jesus from coming back. Jesus told the Jews, "Until you say blessed is He who comes in the name of the Lord, you will not see Me again" (Matt. 23:39). If the Jews do not call on Jesus' name, He will not return. But they do, and He does return (Zech. 9:9, 10:6). Shortly after the antichrist arrives on the scene, the Jews, who had previously rejected Jesus will plea for mercy (Zech. 12:10), and God will respond by pouring out grace on them and by judging this, 'Worthless shepherd' (the antichrist and those following him), once and for all (Zech. 11:17, Rev. 19:19-20).

The passage's application is that Israel's failure, then and now, is also shared by the church. The passage picks up explicitly on three faults for Israel's leaders: 1). Being caught up in their own glory (Zech. 11:3); 2). Loving money (Zech. 11:5, 12-13); and 3). Although they had seen Jesus and knew the word, they rejected Him (Zech. 11:11). The seven churches of the book of Revelation (representing all, collectively through the entire church age) were likewise pre-warned about the same. The book of Revelation starts similarly to the book of Zachariah, with the introduction of God/Jesus (Zech. 1:2, Rev. 1:4-18), stating He is coming back (Zech. 2:10, Rev. 1:7, 8), with a call to Repent, and or Hold Fast (Zech. 1:3, Rev. 2-3). The book of Revelation then goes on to reveal the things to come (Zech. 1-14, Rev. 1:1, 6-19), listing and describing the events throughout the prophecy, as foretold through the prophet Zechariah, starting with the horsemen (Zech. 1:7-21, 6:1-8, Rev. 6:1-8).

In the same way, God warned Israel of pending disaster, Jesus has warned and is warning the church today. In the same way, Israel was judged and will be again, and so will many from within the church will also be judged. Moreover, church leaders who fail in their responsibilities will be severely judged (1 Tim. 1:7, Jam. 3:1), like Israel's failed leaders (Zech. 10:3).

In the same way, God's anger was hot against the shepherds who traded the sheep for greedy gain and traded Jesus for the same, even detesting Him and exchanging Him for the antichrist. Likewise, His anger is hot against failing pastors, conditioning the flock for the coming 'Foolish' and 'Worthless shepherd'. Like Israel's shepherds, many within the church today have bought, sold, and traded the sheep for material gain. They have merchandised God, and the people of God, saying, "Blessed be the Lord, I have become rich" (Zech. 11:5, cf. Rev. 3:17), having no pity for the flock they fleece. In the same way, they have had no compassion for those they plunder; Jesus, whom they claim made them rich, will not pity them.

CHAPTER TWELVE—PART ONE

A CUP OF STAGGERING

'Against All Odds'
(Zech. 12:1-9)

The opening words of chapter twelve are purposed to remind the reader that what God said He will do; He is able to do it. Against all odds, God's word will be fulfilled. God will deliver His people and strike the nations troubling them. Alongside verse one, Isaiah (Isa. 48:12-22) should be compared. God will perform His purpose (Isa. 48:14).

"I am about to make Jerusalem a cup of staggering..." (Zech. 12:2). Verse two of Zechariah chapter twelve is likened to reading a 21st Century newspaper; only, this time, God is the One making the threats, not Iran, and Co. Death threats against Israel have been ongoing since 1948, but the day is coming, and, in fact, the day is nearly here, where God will put an end to the empty rhetoric.

On That Day. The phrase, "On That Day" is mentioned five times in this chapter (Zech. 12:3, 4, 6, 8, 9), three more times in chapter thirteen (Zech. 13:1, 2, 4), and seven more times in chapter fourteen (Zech. 12:4, 6, 8, 9, 13, 21, 22), indicating the significance of it. "That day" will be a day unlike any other, either before or after. The same is true of the events leading up to it and during the seven years of tribulation (Jer. 30:7, Dan. 12:1, Matt. 24:21, Rev. 16:18).

Again, contrary to today's (empty) threats towards Israel from its Arab neighbours, it is they who will be slaughtered on 'That Day', not Israel. And, God orchestrates the event, having also prepared Jerusalem for it, by making her a heavy stone. On That Day, any who try to lift 'that stone' will themselves be hurt (Zech. 12:3). In short, the nation's efforts to remove (lift) Israel (Zech. 12:3) from her place will themselves be lifted (removed) by God. God, not Israel, will strike them down (Zech. 12:4-5), although He will do so in partnership with Israel, having strengthened her (Zech. 12:6-7, 12) for That Day with advanced weaponry and combat skills. As seen through the previous chapters, during the tribulation, God wields Israel like a warrior's sword (Zech. 9:13), devouring their enemies (Zech. 9:15). The prophet predicted that in the last days, God will transform Israel into a mighty warrior (Zech. 10:7), and He has. Today Israel has one of the most advanced defence forces on the planet.

The day of God's judgement against the nations troubling Israel prophetically describes modern weapons of warfare. They were revealed in verse six (Zech. 12:6). Israel's enemies will be burnt up like wood in a blazing fire. At the same time, Jerusalem will be unharmed and unmoved (Zech. 12:3).

On That Day, God will protect Israel, shielding her against all enemies, even sending an angel before her (Zech. 12:8). The reference to the angel should remind us of Sodom and Gomorrah (Gen. 19), and likewise the words of Jesus in the gospel of Luke (Lu. 17:27-29), "People were eating and drinking, marrying and being given in marriage, up to the day Noah entered the ark. Then the flood came and destroyed them all. It was the same in the days of Lot: People were eating and drinking, buying and selling, planting, and building. But on the day Lot left Sodom, fire and brimstone rained down from heaven and destroyed them all."

The concluding sentence, "On That Day... fire and brimstone rained down from heaven," parallels Zachariah's prophecy (Zech. 12:6). God rains down fire from heaven on Israel's enemies, which also describes advanced weapons, seen again in chapter fourteen (Zech. 14:12). Accordingly, this future battle is further described in the fourteenth chapter (Zech. 14:1-3) and the book of Revelation (Rev. 16:16, 19:19), and prophesied elsewhere (cf. Isa. 51:17, 21–22; Jer. 25:15–28).

Against all the odds, the gathering nations set on destroying Israel will be annihilated. The event and outcome will be like the Six-Day War (1967) yet that will be dwarfed by comparison. Furthermore, the reference to God "Striking every horse and its rider" (Zech. 12:4) is mentioned again in chapter fourteen (Zech. 14:15). The prophet previously introduced the red horse of war in chapter one, and again, the four horses of the apocalypse in chapter six, which are the same as in Revelation chapter six.

The red horse of war is further seen in Revelation chapter nine, numbering two-hundred million mounted troops, and they are responsible for slaughtering a third of humankind (Rev. 9:18). Their campaign will lead them towards Jerusalem, specifically, Megiddo, where the battle of Armageddon takes place. There, the cup Jesus drank (Matt. 26:39) is poured out on the warring nations (Jer. 10:25, Rev. 16:1) On That Day!

On that day, God will confuse both horse and rider, causing panic (Zech. 12:4, 14:15), also predicted by Ezekiel (Ezek. 39:9-11). Ezekiel's prophesised Gog of the land Magog war (Ezek. 38-39) occurs at the latter end of the tribulation where the kings of the north invade Israel (Dan. 11:40-45). In the, "Latter years/days" (Ezek. 38:8, 16), "On that day" (Ezek. 38:10, 14, 39:11), the northern armies (Ezek. 38:15, 39:2) (Russia, Turkey), joined by the east (Persia/Iran), the south (Cush/Sudan, Egypt and Ethiopia) and the west (Put/Libya) (Ezek. 38:14-16) will "Advance (against Israel)… like a storm" (Ezek. 38:9). The motivation for the attack is to plunder Israel's goods (Ezek. 38:12-13). The antichrist will counterattack the invading armies, albeit unsuccessfully (Dan. 11:40-45).

At the end of the tribulation, Jesus will deal with the attacking armies, accompanied by an earthquake, hailstones, fire, and sulphur (Ezek. 38:18-23, 39:6). Whatever is left of the dead will be food for the birds and beasts of the field (Ezek. 39:4, 17-20). The book of Revelation picks up on the same prophecy. Revelation chapter sixteen talks about the kings of the east crossing the Euphrates River, met by the kings of the whole world, to assemble at Armageddon (Rev. 16:12-16). Once assembled, Jesus will announce Himself (Rev. 16:17), followed by an earthquake like none other (Rev. 16:18), splitting the city into three parts (Rev. 16:19). God will then stone the rebellious with great hailstones (Rev. 16:21) and cut them down with the sword (Rev. 19:21). Then Jesus will feed their bodies to the birds of the air (Rev. 19:17-18, 21).

While the above-mentioned seems far-fetched, soon, 'On that day', the One who, "Stretched out the heavens and founded the earth and formed the spirit of man within him" (Zech. 12:1) will fulfil His word. As stated through the prophets Zechariah, Jerusalem will become a cup of staggering to all the surrounding peoples (Zech. 12:2). It will become a, "Heavy stone for all the peoples" (Zech. 12:3). Not just the surrounding nations, but, "All the nations of the earth will gather against" Jerusalem (Zech. 12:3, cf. Rev. 16:12-16). God will respond, through His strengthened people (Zech. 12:5), "Devouring to the left and the right all the surrounding people" (Zech. 12:6). In partnership with Israel, God will destroy the nations that come against Jerusalem (Zech. 12:9).

Once the invading nations have been destroyed, then God will re-establish Jerusalem (Zech. 12:6b) and Judah (Zech. 12:7). After that, none will threaten Jerusalem again (Zech. 12:8). None will threaten her again due to Jesus ruling and reigning from the very location with an iron rod. As mentioned previously, the destruction of the nations occurs at the end of the tribulation, followed by the time of peace, the millennial dispensation.

What the prophet Zechariah describes is also picked up by David (Ps. 2). Right now, the nations (intentionally or unintentionally) rage against God (Ps. 2:1), even thinking they can overthrow Him (and His Law) (Ps. 2:3). Still, God laughs at their folly (Ps. 2:4). Soon He will "Speak" and "Terrify them" (Ps. 2:5). Jesus will then, "Break them with a rod of iron and dash them in pieces like a potter's vessel" (Ps. 2:9). Following the judgement of the Gentiles, God will establish His King (Jesus) on, "Zion" the "Holy hill" (Ps. 2:6) where Israel will be His heritage and the end of the earth His possession (Ps. 2:8). Everything the nations claimed to be theirs will be taken from them and redistributed at the commencement of the millennium, at God's discretion (Hag. 2:6-8). "The wealth of the wicked is stored up for the righteous" (Prov. 13:22).

Psalm two and Zechariah chapter twelve speak into the same event. However, David ends the prophecy with a warning, "Now, therefore, O kings, be wise; be warned, O rulers of the earth. Serve the Lord with fear and rejoicing, with trembling. Kiss the Son, lest He be angry, and you perish in the way, for His wrath is quickly kindled. Blessed are all who take refuge in Him" (Ps. 2:10-12). The warning extends to all the nations of the earth, including Israel. The book of Zechariah starts with the same, "Return to Me and [then] I will return to you (Zech. 1:3). If not, then God will do the same to you [Judah] as He did to your forefathers (Zech. 1:4-5), whom He was very angry with" (Zech. 1:2).

As mentioned, many times before, Judah/Israel never truly responded; therefore, they have been temporarily blinded. However, they will be the first to have their eyes opened during the tribulation (Rom. 11:25), followed by countless millions from every nation (Rev. 7:9). Many will join themselves to Jesus through the testimony of the Jews during the tribulation (Zech. 2:11). Many more will remain in rebellion, thereby are the subject of God's anger (Zech. 1:15) and will be destroyed.

"Serve the Lord with fear and rejoicing, with trembling. Kiss the Son, lest He be angry, and you perish in the way, for His wrath is quickly kindled. Blessed are all who take refuge in Him" (Ps. 2:10-12).

CHAPTER TWELVE—PART TWO

ON THAT DAY

'Grace and Mercy'
(Zech. 12:10-13:1)

As mentioned formerly, chapter twelve caps the opening chapter. Chapter one introduces the problem - Judah has moved away from God, and the nations are conspiring against them because of their rebellion. Both acts cause God to respond, being very angry with Judah (Zech. 1:2) and exceedingly angry with the nations (Zech. 1:12, 15). Now, in chapter twelve, the question from chapter one, "Then the angel of the Lord said, 'O Lord of hosts, how long will you have no mercy on Jerusalem and the cities of Judah, against which you have been angry these seventy years?'" (Zech. 1:12), is expanded on.

Despite the religious struggles attempting to appease God during the exile (Zech. 7:5), Judah's best efforts fell well short of the mark to attract His grace and mercy. The reason why is because they were wrongly motivated, everything the religious did, they did for themselves, not God (Zech. 7:6). The same is true today with many in the church, even demanding Israel's inheritance, falsely claiming millennial grace and mercy, favor, and blessings (cf. Zech. 1:16-17) for the here and now. Kingdom Now' theology.'

As seen through verses sixteen and seventeen in chapter one, God's grace and mercy are poured out on the house of David and the inhabitants of Jerusalem (Zech. 12:10), being the Jews, in the millennium. The church is not the house of David or even spiritual Zion. The house of David was first referenced in verse seven (Zech. 12:7), signifying the 'Salvation' of the Jews. Five times the prophet mentioned David (Zech. 12:7, 8, 10, 12, 13:1). During the tribulation, God will strengthen, protect (Zech. 12:8) and save His people, who are the people of David. In a time of trouble, like David (cf. Ps. 32), the Jews will plead for God's mercy and be saved (Zech. 12:12, 13:1). During the tribulation, the Jews, "Return to God" (Zech. 1:3), whereas most from the other nations do not (cf. Ps. 51).

While the passage's immediate context refers to Judah in connection with rebuilding the second temple, immediately following the establishment of the last millennial temple, Jerusalem will overflow with prosperity; God will comfort Zion (Israel) and again choose Jerusalem (Zech. 1:16-17). Since the first temple (Solomon's temple), Israel has not and will not experience peace and prosperity as described in this passage and many more passages like it.

Again, the direct and immediate application of the passage involves rebuilding the second temple; however, the promise of peace and prosperity will not be experienced until the millennial temple is built. Before then, war must come first (Zech. 1:18-21). While many lay claims to the promised millennial blessings of God, neither Israel nor most within the church have any concept of the things to come or the prophetic timeline ending in peace and prosperity.

As mentioned earlier, as Israel did, the church, by and large, falsely claims the future inheritance today, even replacing Israel with themselves as 'Spiritual Israel'. The false doctrine of the church replacing Israel is called 'Replacement theology', subscribed to by charismatics promoting 'Kingdom Now' theology. Kingdom now theology (it is not theology, it is idiocy) is also known as 'Reconstructionism' and 'Dominionism', which is otherwise known as the 'Seven Mountain Mandate'. The seven-mountain mandate teaches that Christians are to dominate the seven mountains of influence, controlling the world in preparation for Jesus' return. That is to acquire peace and prosperity here and now (hence, Kingdom Now). Therefore, God's grace is taught to be directly applied to the seven-mountain mandate, sufficient to achieve (cf. 2 Cor. 12:9).

The seven mountains to be controlled are family, religion, education, media, entertainment, business, and government. The obvious problem with the false teaching of Dominionism (yet not so evident for biblically illiterate charismatics) is that until Jesus returns, Satan is the, "God of this world" (2 Cor. 4:4) and the "Ruler" of it (Jn. 12:31), not Christians, no matter how much they foolishly. 'Name it and claim it'.

Replacement theology is the root cause for many heresies within the church today, including the prosperity-driven seven-mountain mandate and the rejection of the rapture. While dominionists believe things are getting better and better and that Jesus will return to a perfect, dominated world, subdued by Christians, the scripture plainly states that Israel will go through great tribulation (Jer. 30:7, Dan. 12:1, Matt. 24:21) before their Messiah sets up the millennial kingdom. During that time, the Jews, not the church, will flee Judea (Matt. 24:15, cf. Rev. 12). following the antichrist's announcement that he is God (2 Thess. 2:4).

Countering the antichrist during the tribulation are the 144,000 Jewish evangelists (Rev. 17, 4:1-5), not the church, and the two Jewish witnesses (Rev. 11). These are probably Elijah (Mal. 4:5) and Moses (Rev. 15:3) who appeared together at the mount of transfiguration (Matt. 17). The miracles performed by the two witnesses (Rev. 11:4-6)) are only ever seen before in the Old Testament, performed by God through Moses and Elijah. Such miracles have never been seen in the church age, not in 2000 years.

Further to those as mentioned above, nowhere in the book of Revelation is the church revealed in the tribulation. However, if the church has indeed replaced Israel, then the church would go through the tribulation. Conversely, the scripture shows that the church will be removed (taken out of the way) before the tribulation commences (Lu. 21:34-36, 1 Thess. 1:10, 4:16-17, 5:9, 2 Thess. 2:6-8, Rev. 3:10, 4:1). If any from the church find themselves in the tribulation, it will be because they were not saved from the wrath to come; therefore, they were not born again. Many attending churches, calling themselves Christians, will wake up to this reality (cf. Matt. 7:21-23). They will be left behind due to lacking repentance, following doctrines of demons (1 Tim. 4:1, cf. 2 Thess. 2:10-11), and having itching ears, unable to endure sound biblical doctrine (2 Tim. 4:3). Dominionism, incorporating replacement theology, is far from being sound biblical doctrine. If anything, it falls under the category of doctrines of demons. Here and now, salvation, not prosperity, is the principal thing!

While lasting peace and prosperity, through grace and mercy, are inherited in the millennial dispensation, the offerings this side of Christ's return, particularly within the church age, refer to salvation, confirmed by Paul: "We appeal to you not to receive the grace of God in vain. For He says, "In a favorable time I listened to you, and in a day of salvation I have helped you." Behold, now is the favorable time; behold, now is the day of salvation (2 Cor. 6:1-2). By responding to God, ('Drawing near to Him'), salvation is gained through Christ alone. When a sinner comes to Jesus, they get Jesus, not health, wealth, and happiness, not dominion and rule. Again, the latter comes later, in the millennial dispensation. In this age, Jesus said, "You will have tribulation" (Jn. 16:33).

As seen above, due to misunderstanding the biblical prophetic timeline and mishandling (twisting) scripture, the message of grace and mercy is misused and abused to support, "To do, to be and to have" in this life (Your Best Life Now). But here, in Zechariah chapter twelve, among many other places, the prophet provides the proper application through the introduction of sin and suffering, leading to supplication, and repentance, with mourning, when coming face to face with the Living God, "On that day" (Zech. 12:9). "On the day" (Zech. 12:11), immediately after the tribulation (Matt. 24:29), the whole world will come face to face with the visible Christ (Matt. 24:30, Rev. 1:7).

While Zechariah's prophecy is aimed at Judah, who mourns at Christ's appearance (Zech. 12:10), scripture includes the whole world (Matt. 24:30, Rev. 1:7), referring to those left behind to endure the tribulation. Those who survive the seven-year ordeal then face the living, returned God, Jesus Christ.

Addressing sin, the passage and the prophet takes into view Jesus Christ, "Whom they pierced" (Zech. 12:10). Again, supporting the post-tribulation view, the prophet is not so much taking into consideration the crucifixion of Jesus but instead looks well past that event, even two-thousand years further-on, to the return of Jesus after the tribulation. This understanding is reinforced through verse eleven, "On that Day" (Zech. 12:11).

The day referenced is the same that Jesus concluded His Olivet Discord (Matt. 24) with (Matt. 24:30) being the number one sign of the times (Matt. 24:3). While Jesus listed several signs leading to His return, none will be more confronting and frightening than His actual return (Matt. 24:30). When Jesus returns, the whole world, not just Israel, will mourn! Not some, all! All the tribes of the earth will mourn (Matt. 23:30). Jesus' words and warning echo that of the prophet Zechariah (Zech. 12:12). While Israel mourns their sin, the world mourns at the fearful expectation of judgement. The image of the coming judgement, relating to Jesus, was first seen by John, which terrified him (Rev. 1:17). Daniel saw something of the same, albeit unaware of Jesus Christ, causing him to repent for his sins, and the sins of the nation (Dan. 9).

Again, while Zechariah predicts that when Jesus returns, Israel will mourn, John (Rev. 1:7), like Jesus (Matt. 24:30), states the whole earth will mourn. Here, we are reminded of Jeremiah's words, "What will you do when the end comes?" (Jer. 5:31). What will they do?… The righteous will beg for grace and mercy, and the wicked flee, that is what they will do!

While the world mourns in terror of expected judgement, believing Israel and anyone else trusting in Jesus (Zech. 2:11, Rev. 12:17) will be comforted, receiving grace and mercy. As mentioned previously, even at this last stage of the tribulation, in fact, after the tribulation (Matt. 24:29), Jesus affords an opportunity to be saved (Zech. 12:10) by being cleansed from all sin (Zech. 13:1). Those who respond in the required way to Christ's invitation enter the Millennium (Zech. 14:16, cf. Rev. 22:17). Those who do not respond positively, perish.

As mentioned previously, throughout prophetic literature, That Day always refers to Jesus' second coming and the judgement accompanying His return. Everyone who had previously rejected and is rejecting Jesus will recognise Him on that day. The event will take place at the plain of Megiddo (Zech. 12:11b), which is the location of the Battle of Armageddon. The Battle of Armageddon is further described in chapter fourteen of Zechariah and the book of Revelation, chapters sixteen (Rev. 16:14-16) and nineteen (Rev. 19:11-21).

During the tribulation, many Jews will come to faith in Jesus (Rev. 7, 14), bringing about a mass revival, converting multitudes from every nation, all tribes, peoples, and languages (Rev. 7:9). The tribulation revival will be ongoing throughout its seven years, concluding with Jesus' return.

Again, due to God's extended grace and mercy, people will still be able to repent, leading to Jesus' return. To reiterate, according to verse ten, even when Jesus is seen with the naked eye, at His appearing, salvation is still on offer (Zech. 12:10).

As seen in verses ten to fourteen (Zech. 12:10-14), at the appearance of Jesus (Zech. 12:10), an individual response is required through repentance and mourning. Such a response secures salvation, confirmed by chapter thirteen, verse one, "Where comes the cleansing of sin and uncleanness" (Zech. 12:12-14). The applied meaning is that forgiveness is granted to repentant sinners because of God's grace and mercy, also confirmed by Peter (2 Peter 3:9).

In sum, the appearance of Jesus is expanded on further in the book of Revelation (Rev. 1:7), "He is coming with the clouds, and every eye will see Him— even those who pierced Him. Moreover, all the tribes of the earth will mourn because of Him. So shall it be! Amen." The word 'mourning' seen in Zachariah twelve, verse eleven, and Revelation (Rev. 1:7), is eschatological and contextually supports the phrase "On that Day," indicating, again, when this event takes place.

On the return of Jesus, contrary to the response of those revealed through the Revelation/tribulation sixth seal (Rev. 6:14-17), who call for the rocks to fall on and hide them from the Lamb, multitudes collectively and individually plead for grace and mercy and are saved. This is made evident by the words 'Families' and 'Wives' and by 'Themselves', suggesting many will still come to faith in Jesus, through genuine repentance, even at His appearing (Zech. 12:12-14).

In conclusion: The phrase, "On that day" (Zech. 12:11), as seen again in chapter thirteen, verse one, serves as bookends for the passage (Zech. 12:3-13:1). That day refers to none other than the coming day of Jesus Christ (cf. Zech. 14:1). The phrase, 'On that day' occurs sixteen times in these three closing chapters (Zech. 12:3–4, 6, 8–9, 11; 13:1–2, 4; 14:4, 6, 8–9, 13, 20–21) and primarily, but not only, targets the Jews. When Jesus was crucified, He opened salvation to the entire world; now, He narrows in on His original people, Israel. Still, however, the Gentiles are included (Zech. 2:11). On the return of Jesus Christ, all the tribes of the earth will mourn because of Him (Matt. 24:30, Rev. 1:7), implying judgement will be the experience for most, moreover, grace and mercy, resulting in salvation.

CHAPTER THIRTEEN

THE SHEPHERD STRUCK

'The Lord is My God'
(Zech. 13:1-9)

The phrase, 'On that Day', as previously mentioned, is seen sixteen times from chapter twelve through to the end of Zechariah's book, being chapter fourteen (Zech. 12:3–4, 6, 8–9, 11; 13:1–2, 4; 14:4, 6, 8–9, 13, 20–21). Throughout the book of Zechariah, like most other places, the phrase, 'On that Day' always refers to the return of Jesus. In chapter thirteen, the prophet picks up again from chapters ten, verse three (Zech. 10:3), and verse eleven (Zech. 13:11), where 'On that Day' God threatens to judge every false and failing prophet and the foolish shepherds (cf. Zech. 11:15).

Like the previous chapters, alongside the threat of destruction, there is also the promise of cleansing. The cleansing refers to cleansing the land and the people of the land from sin (Zech. 13:1-2). Clearly, the land of Israel has not been cleansed from sin before now; therefore, it will only be cleansed when Jesus returns, judges the nations, and sets up the millennial kingdom 'On that Day'. When Jesus appears, He will then clear out every false person and cleanse every corrupt practice, which includes the removal of past and current pretenders, phonies, and prosperity pimps (prophets/priests/pastors/teachers/tele-evangelists). Furthermore, the cleansing will include the removal of temple relics and the cleansing of temple items used in religious rituals (Zech. 14:20-21). But ultimately, when Jesus returns, the cleansing is aimed at removing the future foolish (Zech. 11:15) and worthless shepherd (Zech. 11:17), the antichrist to come, who will rule for seven years during the tribulation period. (Dan. 9:27; 11:31; Matt. 24:15; 2 Thess. 2:4; Rev. 13:4). The antichrist who directs and authorises the tribulation temple built takes his seat in it (2 Thess. 2:4).

Interestingly, within the passage, Zechariah chapter thirteen, there is a reference to the "Struck Shepherd" (Zech. 13:7) which can easily be mistaken for the antichrist, who is struck in the tribulation (Rev. 13:3, 12, 14). However, the verse refers to Jesus Christ. Jesus is the Good and Faithful Shepherd (Zech. 11:4-14, Rev. 7:17). At the same time, the antichrist is the foolish, worthless shepherd (Zech. 11:15, 17). Jesus Christ is the Lion from the tribe of Judah (Rev. 5:5), coming on a white horse (Rev. 19:11-21), while the antichrist is the lion (Gen. 49:9, Rev. 13:2) from the tribe of Dan (Gen. 49:16-17, Deut. 33:22, Jer. 8:16), coming on a white horse (Rev. 6:2). Both Jesus Christ and the antichrist appear as a lamb (Jn. 1:9, Rev. 13:8, 11); however, the antichrist is a wolf, dressed in sheep's clothing (Matt. 7:15), like the false prophets, who are also, "Servants of Satan" (2 Cor. 10:13-15). Other similarities include, Jesus Christ and the antichrist who perform great signs and wonders, including being resurrected from the dead (Matt. 28:1-20; Mk. 16:1-20; Lu. 24:1-49; and Jn. 20:1-21:25. cf. Rev. 11:7, 17:8, 11). Through the comparisons made, clearly, the antichrist, like Christ, is a literal man, not merely a Beast system as some suggest, albeit the beast system (Ten Kings - New World Order) will accompany him.

Again, the antichrist to come is of Jewish heritage, from the tribe of Dan (Gen. 49:16). No other Jewish king has ever come from the tribe of Dan. The antichrist is the prophesied king, yet to come, rising from the seventh kingdom, forming the eighth (Rev. 17:11). The seventh kingdom is the New World Order (Dan. 7:24, Rev. 17:12-13), being the Revived Roman Empire (Dan. 2:44-45 7:17-18).

Note that in the book of Revelation, the 144,000 Jewish evangelists are made up of 12,000 from each of the twelve tribes (Rev. 7:4-8). The tribe of Dan, like Ephraim, is not mentioned, replaced by Joseph. There are thirteen tribes in Israel. Jacob bore twelve sons, but later, Jacob adopted Joseph's two sons in place of Joseph after moving to Egypt. However, since there is no literal tribe of Joseph, in a sense, we could say that Dan and Ephraim were 'Hidden' in Joseph. If so, then the 12,000 men of the tribe of Joseph in the tribulation will be Danites and Ephraimites.

While scripture reveals that the antichrist is from the tribe of Dan (Gen. 49:16-17, Deut. 33::22) Jer. 8:11-17), Daniel discloses the antichrist will appear from a Gentile region, the, "Great Sea" (Dan. 7:2), which is the Mediterranean region. Therefore, the antichrist will be of Jewish descent, yet he will rise from Gentile land. Genesis is the first place supporting the claim that the antichrist will be of the tribe of Dan. "Dan shall judge his people as one of the tribes of Israel. Dan shall be a serpent in the way, a viper by the path, that bites the horse's heels so that his rider falls backward" (Gen. 49:16-17). Modern artists use the 'Scales of justice', a pagan symbol, to represent the tribe of Dan due to Genesis (Gen. 49:16), referencing Dan judging his people. Dan is also symbolised as a serpent (Gen. 49:17, Jer. 8:17).

The word Dan, in Hebrew, comes from the root for judgement (Heb. Din), meaning to judge and or govern. To date, Dan has never judged, or governed over his brothers, the people of Israel; therefore, the prophecy

(Gen. 49:16-17) is still yet to be fulfilled and will be through the coming antichrist, God's, "Worthless shepherd" (Zech. 11:17). Like the antichrist to come, the Danites were very cunning (2 Chron. 2:13-14), and relate to Bethel (false worship, see chapter seven of this work), being exceedingly idolatrous (1 Kgs. 10:29, 12:28-30). It is due to Dan's idolatry that they are not mentioned in the book of Revelation (Rev. 7:4-8).

The suggestion that the antichrist will come from the tribe of Dan is not new. Irenaeus taught the same, saying, "The blood of Dan will flow through the views of the antichrist." Irenaeus was born in A.D. 130 and died in 202. He was a disciple of Polycarp, a disciple of John (the same John who wrote the book of Revelation). The teachings of Irenaeus are considered among the most important of early Christianity. The fact that Irenaeus was directly discipled by Polycarp, who was a disciple of John, cannot be understated.

Regarding the antichrist, Irenaeus wrote, "These men, therefore, ought to learn [what really is the state of the case] and go back to the true number of the name, that they be not reckoned among false prophets. But, knowing the sure number declared by Scripture, that is, six hundred sixty and six, let them await, in the first place, the division of the kingdom into ten. Then, in the next place, when these kings are reigning, and beginning to set their affairs in order, and advance their kingdom, [let them learn] to acknowledge that he who shall come claiming the kingdom for himself, and shall terrify those men of whom we have been speaking, having a name containing the aforesaid number, is truly the abomination of desolation. This, too, the apostle affirms, "When they shall say, Peace and safety, then sudden destruction shall come upon them." And Jeremiah does not merely point out his sudden coming, but he even indicates the tribe from which he shall come, where he says, 'We shall hear the voice of his swift horses from Dan; the whole earth shall be moved by the voice of the neighing of his galloping horses: he shall also come and devour the earth, and the fullness thereof, the city also, and they that dwell therein.' This, too, is the reason that this tribe is not reckoned in the Apocalypse along with those which are saved.'" [Irenaeus Against Heresies, Book V, p. 1117].

Interestingly, alongside Irenaeus quoting Paul (1 Thess. 5:3), John (Rev. 13:18), and Jesus (Matt. 24:15), Irenaeus also quotes Jeremiah (Jer. 8:11-17). Jeremiah's prophecy captures both the invasion of Jerusalem from the Babylonians and the antichrist to come, as seen through verses sixteen and seventeen of Jeremiah's prophecy (Jer. 11:16-17), "The snorting of their horses is heard from Dan, at the sound of the neighing of their stallions the whole land quakes. They devour the land and all that fills it, the city and those who dwell there. For behold, I am sending among you serpents, adders that cannot be charmed, and they shall bite you," declares the Lord."

Through the writings of Irenaeus, the reader can clearly see he had no problem linking the, "Abomination of desolation" (Matt. 24:15) with the time of "Peace and security" (1 Thess. 5:3), and the snorting horses of Dan (Jer. 11:16). It concludes that Irenaeus perceives the tribe of Dan to be the ancestors of the serpent seed, the antichrist.

The snorting horses heard from Dan can be linked to Revelation, chapter (Rev. 6:2), and the book of Zechariah (Zech. 1:7-17, 6:1-8). As mentioned in the previous section, the tribulation primarily aims at Israel. The church does not go through the time of trouble (1 Thess. 5:9, Rev. 3:10). The purpose of the tribulation is to deal with Israel's pride, which has temporarily blinded them (cf. Rom. 11). During that seven-year ordeal, "Dan will judge Israel" (Gen. 49:16). Israel will be tested in the, "Hour of trial that is coming on the whole of the world, to try those who dwell on the earth" (Rev. 3:10).

An interesting side note, also seen through the writings of Irenaeus (Irenaeus Against Heresies), is that he holds to premillennialism (AH.

5:35). He believes in a pre-tribulation rapture (AH. 5:29), followed by the resurrected (Revived) Roman Empire (AH. 5:30) that is made up of ten nations (AH. 5:26). Also, as in the church age, leading into the tribulation where there will be a great falling away (2 Thess. 2:3), Irenaeus believes it will be the same for Israel during the time of testing (Matt. 24:5, 10-12, 24), especially once the third temple is built (Matt. 24:15).

The reconstruction of the third temple is the sign commencing the middle of Daniel's seventieth week (Dan. 9:24-27) where the antichrist, from the tribe of Dan (AH. 5:30), will announce himself to be God (AH. 5:25). The middle of the week is the great tribulation, a time like never seen before or will be again (Jer. 30:7, Dan. 12:1, Matt. 24:21). At that time, the antichrist will be recognised by the number of his name, 666 (AH. 5:30), by those having wisdom (Rev. 13:18). The wise will understand (Dan. 12:10), "From the time that the regular burnt offering is taken away and the abomination that makes desolation is set up, there shall be 1,290 days" (Dan. 12:11). One thousand two hundred ninety days is three and a half years (the halfway point of the tribulation), plus (I believe) a thirty-day interval for the commissioning of the third temple. There is another forty-five-day interval when Jesus returns to decommission the third temple, cleanse the land (Zech. 13:2) and commission the fourth temple (Dan. 12:12). One thousand three hundred thirty-five days (Dan. 12:12) refers to the three and a half years (1260-days) following the third temple construct, the abomination of desolation, and the return of Jesus Christ, with forty-five days remaining.

Adding to Irenaeus is Hippolytus, a student and disciple of Irenaeus, who lived from A.D. 170 to A.D. 236. In agreement with his teacher on the antichrist's Danite background, Hippolytus writes, "Thus did the Scriptures preach before-time of this lion and lion's whelp. And in like manner also we find it written regarding antichrist. For Moses speaks thus:

'Dan is a lion's whelp, and he shall leap from Bashan.' But that no one may err by supposing that this is said of the Saviour, let him attend carefully to the matter. 'Dan,' he says, 'is a lion's whelp;' and in naming the tribe of Dan, he clearly declared the tribe from which antichrist is destined to spring. For as Christ springs from the tribe of Judah, so antichrist is to spring from the tribe of Dan. And that the case stands thus, we see also from the words of Jacob: 'Let Dan be 'a serpent, lying upon the ground, biting the horse's heel.' What, then, is meant by the serpent but antichrist, that deceiver who is mentioned in Genesis, who deceived Eve and supplanted Adam? But since it is necessary to prove this assertion by sufficient testimony, we shall not shrink from the task. That it is in reality out of the tribe of Dan, then, that that tyrant and king, that dread judge, that son of the devil, is destined to spring and arise, the prophet testifies when he says, 'Dan shall judge his people, as (he is) also one tribe in Israel.' But someone may say that this refers to Samson, who sprang from the tribe of Dan, and judged the people for twenty years. Well, the prophecy had its partial fulfillment in Samson, but its complete fulfillment is reserved for antichrist. For Jeremiah also speaks to this effect: 'From Dan we are to hear the sound of the swiftness of his horses: the whole land trembled at the sound of the neighing, of the driving of his horses.'" [The Extant Works and Fragments, Part 2, Paragraph 14].

As seen above, Hippolytus connects the serpent in Dan's prophecy with the serpent in the Garden of Eden. The direct conclusion is that the antichrist is of the seed of the old serpent, Satan. Therefore, the antichrist will fulfill the prophecy concerning the seed of the serpent. Further evidence is seen through Hippolytus' reference to Deuteronomy, "And of Dan he said, Dan is a lion's whelp: he shall leap from Bashan" (Deut. 33:22). The Bashan prophecy confirms that a Lion will come from Dan, proclaiming to be the Messiah, yet will deceive and ultimate judge, or cause Israel, and the rest of the world, to be judged by God (2 Thess. 2:9-12).

During the seven-year event, the antichrist will not only cause Israel to follow him, but multitudes from every nation to worship him (Rev. 9:20, 13:14-17), persecuting any who refuse (Rev. 7:14b, 20:4). Anyone who worships the antichrist, thereby rejecting Jesus Christ, by receiving the beast's Mark (666), will be from that point on (the halfway point), unredeemable, and condemned to the eternal lake of fire (Rev. 14:9-11, 20:11-15).

During the antichrist's rule, the sheep will be scattered (Zech. 1:18-20, 13:7). The prophecy of the scattering of the sheep was partly fulfilled when Jesus was crucified (Isa. 53:4, 7, 10), where the disciples fled (Matt. 26:31, 56). The future scattering of the sheep will take place during the tribulation (Matt. 24:9-12), where even God's 'Little ones' (Zech. 13:7b) will be persecuted for a time, and God will allow it (Zech. 17:17, cf. Rev. 12:13-17). So severe will the persecution be, two-thirds of the Jewish nation will be struck down, with the remaining one-third, purged and purified by the tribulation (Rev. 22:1). The surviving few (Zech. 13:8), who have called on the name of the Lord in faith, and triggered His return (Matt. 23:39), will be cleansed (Zech. 12:10–13:1), and will enter the millennial kingdom (Zech. 14:16).

During the millennial dispensation, those who once practiced falsehood and have since repented will never return to their old ways (Zech. 13:2-6). Returning to the opening verses, "On that Day" (Zech. 13:2a), God will "Cut off the names of the idols from the land. And, remove the prophets and the spirit of uncleanness" (Zech. 13:2b). To remove uncleanness from the land, God, "Will pour out on the house of David and the inhabitants of Jerusalem a spirit of grace and pleas for mercy" (Zech. 12:10). From that day, none will prophesy falsely; if they do, they will die at the hand of their parents (Zech. 13:3). Due to the shame of previously prophesying falsely, those that did will even lie in the millennium to cover it up (Zech. 13:4-6).

In the millennial kingdom, Israel indeed returns to God (Zech. 1:3). At this point, in Jeremiah, chapters eight to ten should be considered, also containing the prophecy mentioned above of Dan judging Israel (Jer. 8:16-17). The language of Jeremiah (chapters 8-10) regarding the false prophets is very similar to that of Zechariah (chapter 13). Before God restores Israel, He will first deal with the, "Everyone, greedy for unjust gain" (Jer. 8:10), "From prophet to priest" (Jer. 10), prophesying, "Peace, peace, when there was no peace" (Jer. 8:11). On that Day, God will pour out His wrath (Jer. 10:25) on the "Shepherds, who are stupid and do not inquire of the Lord" (Jer. 10:21). As mentioned earlier, after the judgement, whatever then is left, whoever survives and submits to Jesus, they will go into the millennial kingdom (Zech. 14:16). On that day, having returned to God, and Him to them (Zech. 1:3) Judah (Israel) will say, "The Lord is my God" (Zech. 13:9).

In sum: On that Day, not only will Jesus cleanse the land of the false and faithless; but even the lying prophets' parents will play a part in doing the same, putting them to death (Zech. 13:3). Following the judgement referenced by 'That Day' (Zech. 13:2) is the millennial reign of Jesus. During the one thousand years of peace, no longer will religious men practice their trade for selfish and greedy gain. No more will they parade around in their religious garb (Zech. 13:4) or promote themselves through 'Self-sacrifice' (Zech. 13:6). But instead, they will hide and even go as far as to lie about their former practices and activities, which resulted in scars (Zech. 13:6) gained from idol worship (whipping rituals). In replacement, they will opt for regular and honest work (Zech. 13:5). Moreover, the failing, false, and phony shepherds, including the antichrist, will be replaced by the One True and Good Shepherd, Jesus (Zech. 11:4-14).

As a side note: Although the tribe of Dan is missing from the book of Revelation, they are seen again in the millennial kingdom (Ezek. 48:1-2, 32). Ezekiel (Ezek. 48:32) provides information regarding their land portion and its position within the millennial kingdom. While they will continue to reject God until the tribulation commences, some will submit to Jesus during it.

In conclusion, during the tribulation, the antichrist, a descendant from the tribe of Dan, will strike the sheep (Israel), scattering them. Triggering the tribulation is the signing of the peace treaty, which is broken after three and a half years (Isa. 26:15, 18, Dan. 9:24-27). Therefore, the antichrist will turn on the Jews from the midway point (Dan. 11:41), when they are saying, "Peace and security (1 Thess. 5:3). At that time, many will fall away from their (Jewish) faith and follow the antichrist (Matt. 24:10-12, 15, 23-27). Many will also falsely prophecy, as they have done before, even in Christ's name (Zech. 13:4-6, cf. Matt. 24:24). During the hour of trial (Rev. 3:10), most will perish; however, a few, just a remnant, will survive, being tested like gold through the fire. The testing is the antichrist's deception and persecution (Zech. 13:8-9a). However, at the end of the tribulation, Jesus Christ will return and strike the antichrist (Dan. 7:11, 26, 11:45b, 2 Thess. 2:8, Rev. 19:20) and those following him (Rev. 6:12-17, 17:14, 19:11-19, 21b). Then, Jesus will cleanse the land and the people of the land. From that day, He will then, once again, be their God, and they (Israel) will be His people, saying, 'The Lord is my God'" (Zech. 13:9).

CHAPTER FOURTEEN

THE DAY OF THE LORD

'The Lord will be King over all the Earth.'
(Zech. 14:1-20)

Out of the sixteen times in the concluding chapters of Zechariah (chapters 12-14), the phrase 'On that Day' is seen eight times within chapter fourteen. That Day describes what is otherwise known as the battle or campaign of Armageddon. For such an occasion, chapter fourteen shows God is the one gathering all the nations (Zech. 14:2) and will be the one fighting against the nations (Zech. 14:4) because of their sin (cf. Zeph. 1:14-18). He will fight against the nations, literally and personally, when He (Jesus) returns after the tribulation (Zech. 14:4-5). Following the tribulation, then the millennial dispensation (Zech. 14:6-11) will commence, bringing with it all the promises of peace and prosperity, namely, knowing (Zech. 8:20-23) and experiencing God (Zech. 2:10-11).

Zechariah, chapter fourteen confirms that when Jesus returns, whatever has been taken from Israel by the nations (Zech. 14:1-3), will be returned when the Land is restored (Zech. 14:6-11, 14, Hab. 2:6-9). As a side note, despite false teaching and songs claiming that believers can take back what the devil has stolen, here and now, referring to health and wealth, there is not a single verse in the Bible that supports that. God restores, first through Christ on the cross, redeeming humanity, and secondly through His return, restoring humanity to its rightful and ruling place alongside Him.

Before Jesus returns, there will be an all-out war, where the nations will appear victorious over Israel, albeit short lasting. When Jesus returns, every eye will see Him, standing on the Mount of Olives (Zech. 14:3, cf. 12:10, Matt. 24:30, Rev. 1:7), splitting it into two halves (Zech. 14:4), as a great earthquake (Zech. 14:5, cf. Rev. 6:12, 16:18-21). No one will miss that event; none will be deceived anymore by the antichrist, proclaiming to be the Messiah when Jesus returns. When Jesus returns, He also proclaims this to the saints (Zech. 14:5, Jude 14, Rev. 19:14); then, most will flee in fear, even hide in caves (Rev. 6:12-17) rather than, "Kiss the Son," that His wrath may be quickly kindled (Ps. 2:12).

As mentioned previously, war must come first before there is lasting peace. Before Christ's rule in the millennial dispensation, the prophet Zechariah narrows in on the plagues that the Lord pours out on the Gentiles at the end of the tribulation (Zech. 14:12). This includes something likened to nuclear warfare, although it will not be a nuke, confirmed by Jesus (Matt. 24:22). If a nuke was used, there would be no human left alive. Still, the plague of God is significant in response to the nations that have troubled Israel, who are, seemingly, at rest, and who God is exceedingly angry with (Zech. 1:12, 15).

As mentioned above, when Jesus returns, the rebels flee. Verse thirteen (Zech. 14:13) reveals why, "On that day, a great panic from the Lord shall fall on them." The predicted response of those rebelling against God should remind us, again, of Jeremiah's words, "What will you do when the end comes?" (Jer. 5:31). John, in the book of Revelation, pens something of the same, "For the great day of their wrath has come, and who can stand?" (Rev. 6:17). The statement, moreover, a question, is answered through Zechariah (Zech. 14:13). When Jesus returns, none, outside of Christ will be able to stand! All outside of Christ will instead be terrified to death, 'On that day'. The very ones who tried to move Jerusalem from its place and remove the people from their land (Zech. 12:3), they will be struck down by God (Zech. 12:4), and their horses (Zech. 12:4), destroying them once and for all (Zech. 14:9).

As seen through chapter twelve, verse four (Zech. 12:4), on that day, the predicted plague will not only destroy God's enemies, but every living creature, as confirmed in chapter fourteen (Zech. 14:15). The destruction of the animals mainly refers to the horses, mules, camels, and donkeys going into battle. Although, "Whatever beast may be in those camps, will be destroyed" (Zech. 14:15b).

The horses destroyed include those of Revelation chapter six (Rev. 6:1-8) and nine (Rev. 9:12-19), mentioned again in chapter nineteen (Rev. 19:18, 21). Zechariah mentions the horses in chapters one (Zech. 1:7-17) and six (Zech. 6:1-8), referring to the four apocalyptic horsemen. Of the remaining few who survive the tribulation (cf. Zech. 13:8-9, 14:2), even less will survive this specific event, the Battle of Armageddon. The few (million) who do will go into the millennium, living under Jesus' rule, which means they are required to worship Him (Zech. 14:16) and Him alone (cf. Rev. 14:7). Still, some will refuse (Zech. 14:16, 17, 18), even then. Therefore, God will respond by shutting off the rain, to begin with (Zech. 14:16).

In the current day, it rains on the just and unjust alike (Matt. 5:45). All are subject to the same, for good and for bad. All can suffer sickness, poverty, and pain similarly, health, wealth, and happiness. There is no exception to this, regardless of whether you are a follower of Jesus or not. In fact, when following Jesus, there is a greater chance of trouble in this life (Jn. 16:33). However, after the tribulation and during the millennial kingdom, God will no longer treat the faithful and unfaithful in the same way.

Remember, there will be no atheists during the tribulation, for even the antichrist curses God (Dan. 7:25) and the saints in heaven (Rev. 13:6). Likewise, in the millennial, the earth will be filled with the knowledge of God (Hab. 2:14) as Jesus will be the visible and ever-present ruling King over the whole world (Zech. 14:9). Again, only those coming to faith in Christ alone, in the tribulation will enter the millennial kingdom, as millennials (Zech. 12:10, 13:1, 14:16). The rest within the kingdom, those returning with Christ, will be glorified. Therefore, there will be no excuse for any who refuses to worship God! But for the ones who do, and they will, not only will God turn off the rain on that day, but He will also revisit the rebels with a plague (Zech. 14:18) of fire coming down from heaven (Rev. 20:9).

As an interesting observation, worship is a central theme throughout the Bible, with two competing forces, God and Satan. During the tribulation, the same is true. The book of Revelation provides thirteen accounts pointing toward worshipping God and eight more referencing those who worship the antichrist. During the millennium, nothing has changed. As mentioned above, some refuse to worship God, even when there is no tempter, as seen in verses twenty and twenty-one (Zech. 14:20-21, cf. Rev. 20:7). For those remaining faithful, worshipping God alone, everything is made new and holy, alongside every practice and every person. The old has gone, and the new has come, entirely and only possible under Christ's rule.

The words, "No longer are there any traders in the house" (Zech. 14:21) confirm that everything stolen has been restored in the name of God. The phrase refers to those who merchandise God and the people of God, such as Jeremiah and Jesus described, indicating they were a company of thieves, a, "Den of Robbers" (Jer. 7:11, Matt. 21:13). Zechariah, chapter thirteen picks up on the same (Zech. 13:2-6) stating, in the millennium, the false prophet will no longer practice his trade (control, and con people off in the name of religion). Chapter ten in the book of Zechariah also states that the shepherds and leaders causing Israel to wander, who God is very angry with (Zech. 1:2), will be dealt with in the tribulation (Zech. 10:3). The failing shepherds caused the people of God to wander due to their deception (false words, lying dreams, and visions), and hypocrisy, saying, "Peace, peace when there is no peace" (Jer. 6:4).

At the end of the tribulation, due to the grace and mercy of God, even the false prophets and failing shepherds, the 'Den of robbers', have an opportunity to enter the millennial kingdom (Zech. 13:4-6), like the nations will (Zech. 2:11), even those who have come against Jerusalem (Zech. 14:1-2). They, too, are invited and allowed to enter the millennium (Zech. 14:16) by looking on the visible Christ and mourning (repenting) over their sin (Zech. 12:10c). Even at the last stage, when Christ appears, God's grace and mercy will be poured out for any to receive. (Zech. 12:10b).

Then, in the millennium, war and the old corrupt religious practices are done away with. Today, the 'Den of robbers' include any using religion and God for greedy gain yet refusing to know, fear, and worship Him. The fraudsters are seen and easily identified, particularly within the megachurches and charismatic movements but will no longer exist in the coming one thousand years of peace. (Zech. 14:18). As mentioned earlier, should they reengage in their old ways, even their parents will put them to death (Zech. 13:3).

Replacing false worship in the millennium is the pure worship of the one true God, known by name (Zech. 14:9). The worship of God (Jesus Christ) is practiced through the 'Feast of Booths'. Three times, this festival is mentioned in Zechariah, chapter fourteen (Zech. 14:16, 18, 19). The

Feast of Booths or Feast of Tabernacles is also known as Sukkot. Sukkot is the final feast, following Yom Kippur, or the Feast of Atonement, which follows Rosh Hashanah, the Feast of Trumpets.

The Feast of Booths takes place on the fifteenth day of Tishrei. Again, Sukkot directly follows Yom Kippur and lasts seven days (Lev. 23:39–40), followed by one more, an eighth day (Lev. 23:36). Sukkot commemorates the forty-year period during which the children of Israel were wandering in the desert and living in temporary shelters; the futuristic millennial dispensation will resemble something of the same (cf. 2 Cor. 5:1). The eighth day will usher in the new heaven and new earth, which will be a permanent dwelling place (Rev. 21—22).

Interestingly, Rosh Hashanah (Feast of Trumpets) is referenced with Israel commencing her journey in the wilderness (Exod. 19:13, 16). At the same time Yom Kippur (Feast of Atonement) can be linked to Moses pleading for forgiveness (Exod. 32:31–32) of Israel's 'Great sin' (Exod. 32:21). So great was the sin of Israel that Moses was unsure whether God would, or even could, forgive her (Exod. 32:32b; 33:16). However, when Moses descends a second time from Mount Sinai some forty days later (Exod. 34:28), the atonement, and thus forgiveness, for the great sin had been granted and realised. The realisation comes through the renewed covenant (Exod. 34:10) and God's manifest, visible glory (Exod. 34:29–35).

The tribulation parallels the Exodus story with the sounding of the trumpet, which sounds as a warning regarding the commencement of the time of trouble (1 Thess. 4:16; Rev. 4:1; cf. 6:1). Again, the time of trouble is set to purge by bringing about repentance (Rev. 9:20–21; 16:9–11). The second feast will determine the response and outcome of the first (Rev. 20:12). Only those who respond to the first feast are found acceptable in the second (Rev. 11:12) and therefore partake of the 'Fixed time' (Col. 2:17) of the third, being that of Sukkot (Rev. 21:3).

Here again, the visible glory of God will be made manifest upon the earth (Rev. 21:3). That is, at the consummation (cf. Luke 5:33–39; Rev. 19:7–9), the whole earth will be filled with His glory (Ps. 72:19; Isa. 6:3; Heb. 2:14). Not since the Mount of Transfiguration (Matt. 17) has God's shekinah glory been made manifest among humankind, despite many movements claiming it through various revivals, healing meetings, and an assortment of other supernatural experiences. Paul's experience on the Damascus Road is the exception to the Mount of Transfiguration manifestation (cf. Acts 8:3–6).

In the millennium, the future glory of God will not be isolated to one place but will fill the whole earth (Num. 14:21; Hab. 2:14). This experience will be greater than anything previously experienced (Hag. 2:9). On that, it is important to note that the future and greater glory verses (Num. 12:21; Hab. 2:14; Hag. 2:9) are millennial references.

Before the Mount of Transfiguration, the shekinah glory of God was made known in the first coming of Christ, according to John (Jn. 1:14), "The Word became flesh and dwelt among us, and we beheld His glory, glory as of the only Son." The exception to the Transfiguration of the Mount manifestation (Matt. 17:1-8; cf. 2 Pet. 1:16–17) is with Christ's resurrection and ascension (see John 17:5; Phil. 2:5–11), and then again with Paul, as mentioned above (Acts 8:3-6).

In the Old Testament, the shekinah glory was made manifest in the Holy of Holies (Exod. 25:22; Lev. 16:2; 2 Sam. 6:2; 2 Kgs. 19:14–15; Psa. 80:1; Isa. 37:16; Ezek. 9:3; 10:18; Heb. 9:5), thus restricted to a select few. So, again, during the millennial, everyone will experience God's glory.

As mentioned earlier, and yet quite unbelievably, in the millennium, although God's glory is made manifest for all to enjoy, and there is an absence of 'traders,' self-worshipping rebels will still abound, making up a vast army of the deceived, blindly following Satan. They will be led by the devil who has been released from the bottomless pit, after one thousand years, to march against Jerusalem. Albeit, their campaign will be short-lasting, and met with fire reigning down from heaven, which will consume them (Zech. 14:18, Rev. 20:7-10). The plague of fire raining down from heaven at the end of the millennium is a repeat of verse twelve (Zech. 14:12), taking place at the end of the tribulation.

Where Zachariah's vision ends (Zech. 14), John's continues six times, referring to the literal one-thousand-year reign (Rev. 20:2, 3, 4, 5, 6, 7). Following the millennium is the judgement at the Great White Throne. Here, the books are opened, and the unjust are resurrected from Hades for everlasting damnation; they are cast eternally into the lake of fire (Rev. 20:11-15). The lake of fire is where the antichrist and false prophet have already been for one thousand years. Note that they have been there for one thousand years and have not one less day to stay!

Contrary to false teaching supporting annihilationism, in replacement of eternal suffering, Revelation, chapter twenty (Rev. 20:10) states that the antichrist and false prophet are tormented day and night forever and ever. The same is true of those worshiping the beast, who has received his Mark (666) (Rev 14:11). In fact, all rejecting Jesus will be resurrected, and following their resurrection, they will be cast into the eternal lake of fire. Again, the resurrected are the unjust, as mentioned by Daniel, John, and Luke (Dan. 12:2b; John 5:28-29b; Acts 24:15b). Upon their resurrection, they, too, will receive a glorified body for everlasting torment. For with the body, they sinned, and with the body, they will suffer (Mark 9:42-48, Matt. 10:28).

Regarding the Book of Life: Revelation, chapters thirteen and seventeen (Rev. 13:8, 17:8) speak of the names of the saved and unsaved written and not written in the Lamb's book of life, "From the foundation of the world." This does not support the false doctrine of predestination taught by Calvinists, where God has predestined some to eternal life and others to destruction. Predestination, instead, is merely stating that God knew from beginning to end who would accept and who would reject Him.

Regarding the Book of Life, Jesus told the church of Sardis that the one who conquers would never be blotted from the Book of Life (Rev. 3:5). The promise is conditional, warning the church members that unless they conquer and hold fast (repent, and remain in a repentance state), then their names will be removed from the Book of Life (Rev. 3:5). The one who conquers is the same as those being tested by fire (Zech. 13:9, 1 Pet. 1:7). No matter what dispensation, God is always testing His people (Gen. 2:16, Deut. 8:2, Heb. 3:8, 12:5-13, 1 Pet. 1:7, Zech. 13:9, 14:17-19), sifting the goats from the sheep, and exposing the wolves. Only the sheep remain.

The book of life is mentioned six times in the book of Revelation (3:5, 13:8, 17:8, 20:12, 20:15, 21:27). With each one comes a warning - unless your name is written in the book, you will be judged by the books, which contain your works outside of Christ. The books containing individual works will be compared alongside the Ten Commandments. Where any have failed and fallen short by breaking the commandments, they will be judged accordingly. James says: "If you fail in one point of the Law, you become accountable for all of it" (Ja. 2:10). Therefore, the failing and the unrepentant person will receive their full reward and inheritance in the lake of fire (Rev. 20:11-15).

Following the judgment, God will create a new heaven and a new earth, as described in Revelation chapters twenty-one and twenty-two (Rev. 21-22). Only those putting their faith in Jesus, by obediently following Him, will inherit eternal life. Remember, the book of Revelation is written to the churches (2-3, 22:16) with a message: Repent and or hold fast until the end. For, "Only those who endure until the end will be saved" (Matt. 24:13).

In conclusion: As Zechariah begins (Zech. 1:3), he ends (13:9). The opening verse of the book starts by calling God's wandering people to return to Him (Zech. 1:3), followed by visions of the coming tribulation (1:7-21, chapters 2-7). Then Israel's redemption and restoration (chapters 8, 10, and 12), proceeded by God's judgement on the nations (chapter 9), and judgement on the failing shepherds (chapters 10, 11 and 13). Finally, the chapters conclude with a focus on Jesus' return and the events following.

When compared alongside the book of Revelation, we see a similar pattern. The churches are warned to repent (return) and hold fast (Rev. 2-3). Following, the events of the tribulation are detailed (Revelation, chapters 6-19), concluding with Jesus' return (Rev. 19), the judgement (Rev. 20), and restoration (Rev. 21-22). The central theme of both books (Zechariah and Revelation) is Jesus, focusing on His return. The book of Revelation places an urgency on getting right with God (Rev 2-3) in preparation for His return (Rev. 1:1b, 3, 7, 22:7, 12, 20), as does Zechariah (Zech. 2:4, 6, 7). The announcement of Jesus' return is made plain (Rev. 1:3, 22:6, 10, 12, and 20), although the event will surprise most sleeping people, catching them off guard. Hence the reason why Jesus warned, "You must be ready!" (Matt. 24:44).

The urgency of the message serves to remind the reader of Zechariah to "Run" (Zech. 2:4), get up, "Up, up" (Zech. 2:6), and "Flee." "Escape" (Zech. 2:7) the judgement to come, "On that day." While the words are contextually aimed at those in the tribulation, they also serve the church here and now. On both accounts, the prepared believer is ready "For the Lord, [who] will be King over all the Earth" (Zech. 14:9).

THE RIDDLE OF TIME

'The Final Countdown'
Ezra Two (2 Esdras)

F ollowing Zechariah, chapter six, which focused on the four chariots (Zech. 6:1-8), and the temple rebuild (Zech. 9-15), Ezra, chapters five and six were considered. The next chapter of Zechariah (chapter 7) addressed false worship (Beware of Bethel), followed by chapter eight revealing lasting peace and prosperity in the millennium.

Ezra chapters five and six are chronologically set with Zechariah, chapter six, where the Jews were instructed to diligently obey (Zech. 6:16). By doing so, it would result in lasting prosperity (Ezra 5:8, 6:14). While Zechariah, chapter six, unbeknownst to him, is focused on the millennial dispensation, where the last temple would exist, Ezra is concentrated in the second temple, yet one leads to the other, albeit two-thousand, five-hundred years apart. Zechariah's vision of the last temple is springboarded from the second (Zech. 4:6-10).

Ezra is an important player in the book of Zechariah, albeit not mentioned, like in the book of Haggai, due to being the one who reintroduces both prophets, encouraging Judah to stay the course (Ezra 5:1-2). Both prophets expected the Messiah to come on the completion of the second temple; unbeknownst to them, their visions reveal the last, millennial temple (Hag. 2:9, Zech.6:11-12). Only here, in the book of Ezra, do we see two prophets standing side-by-side encouraging, not rebuking and warning, the Jews.

While both the prophets Haggai and Zechariah are clearly writing about the tribulation and millennial kingdom, Ezra is not known by most to also have insight into the end times. However, the book of Esdras (2) shows that he does. The book of Esdras (2), or the 'Apocalypse of Ezra', is among the apocryphal books included in the King James 1611 Bible. In the King James 1611 Bible, there are eighteen additional books, called Deuterocanonical books, meaning sacred books or literary works, forming a secondary canon.

The Apocrypha was officially removed in 1885 due to a dispute between the Roman Catholics and the Anglicans. The disagreement was from the Anglicans; however, there is one book that the Anglicans accepted, yet the Catholics rejected, being the Apocalypse of Ezra. While now removed from modern Bibles, Josephus, the historian of the first century A.D., used it in preference to the canonical Ezra–Nehemiah. The "Tale of the Three Guardsmen" includes Esdras's books (1 & 2).

Esdras (2) is twenty-four pages in length, containing sixteen chapters. The prophetic outline is as follows:

1. Israel's disobedience and rejection (1:24:38)
2. The church age (1:33-38)
3. God's judgement in Israel (2)
4. The rapture (2:15-19, 33-38, 42-48)
5. The resurrected (3:42-48)
6. The riddle of time (4:38-52)
7. Signs of the end (5-6:1-25)
8. Children born prematurely shall live and leap about (6:21)

9. The rapture (6:22-29)
10. Messianic kingdom (7:26-43)
11. Great White Throne Judgement (7:36-41)
12. Seven years of tribulation (7:43-44)
13. Only a few will be saved (7:45-61)
14. Many created, few live (8)
15. More signs about the end times (9:1-13)
16. Few saved (9:13-22)
17. The weeping woman, future Zion (10)
18. The vision of the eagle (11)
19. The vision of the eagle interpreted (12)
20. Rapture, tribulation, and the Second Coming (12:31-35)
21. The Messiah, from the sea (13)—Compare with Zechariah chapters twelve to fourteen.
22. The resurrection (14:35-36)
23. The last days (15)
24. The last days continued (16)

Within the book of Esdras (2), there is very little that cannot be found in the Bible, as we have it today, perhaps except for the "Riddle of time" (Esd. 4:38-52). The only reference to the prophetic timeline, outside of Daniel, chapter nine (Dan. 9:24-27), narrowing in on Christ's return in the modern Bible, is Israel's rebirth, called, "The lesion of the fig tree" (Matt. 24:32-35).

Taken from my book *Daniel's Divulgement:*

The final 'week' (Dan. 9:27) or seven years derived from the Hebrew word 'shavuim' would be better translated as 'sevens'. The actual term for 'week' is 'Shavuot'. Again, up until this point, Daniel (Dan. 9:2) expects the Kingdom of God to be established after the seventy weeks (years) of captivity, much like John the Baptist (Matt. 11:3), and the disciples thought that Jesus was going to set up the Kingdom at His first appearance (Lu. 19:11); likewise did the Jews in Jerusalem (Mk. 11:9-10). Daniel misunderstood not only the length of time but the gap in-between, to which God brought correction through His angelic messenger, Gabriel (Dan. 9:22-27).

To reiterate, commencing the "Seven weeks" (tribulation) is the signing of the covenant or peace treaty, 'guaranteeing' seven years of peace (Dan. 9:27). The signing of the peace treaty will coincide with the rebuilding of the third, tribulation, temple. The antichrist, however, will break this covenant halfway through the tribulation (Dan. 9:27; Rev. 11:1- 2). Isaiah predicts the same, calling this false peace treaty a "covenant of death" (Isa. 28:15). In Paul's letter to the Thessalonians, he also mentions it, referencing a perceived time of "Peace and security" before sudden destruction (1 Thess. 5:3). As previously stated, and supported through Paul's writings, the destruction occurs after the rapture (1 Thess. 4:15, 17). Here, the distinction between 'They' (1 Thess. 5:3) and 'Those' (1 Thess. 5:7) from "You, "We" (1 Thess. 5:5, 10), and 'Us' (1 Thess. 5:6, 8, 10) makes it clear. Further support outlining the futuristic timing of this event is found in the book of Revelation, chapter seventeen.

The signing of the Middle East Peace treaty will trigger the tribulation and reveal the antichrist for those who are wise. Currently, there is a peace treaty tabled called, The Abrahamic Accord. With a high level of confidence, we can believe that this current tabled peace treaty will be the one signed by the antichrist, triggering the tribulation, concluding that the time remaining is short.

Further support suggesting the time is short is seen when Jesus taught the disciples, 'when' the branches of the fig tree become tender and put out its leaf, (then) you will know summer is near (Matt. 24:33). Twice Jesus said 'near' (Matt. 24:33, 34). Included with the sign of the fig tree,

Jesus said, "When you see ALL these things (signs), you will know that He (Jesus) is near, at the very gates" (Matt. 24:33). Jesus' reference to 'all these things' includes everything mentioned from verse four onwards (Matt. 24:4-35). Included in the list of signs is the lesson from the fig tree. The fig tree is a significant sign of the end times signs, commencing the visible prophetic countdown. Jesus went on to say, "This generation will not pass away until all these things take place" (Matt. 24:34). It is also important to note Jesus' reference to 'You'. Four times Jesus said, "You will know and see by the signs of the times; you (being the generation that sees the signs) will not pass away until all the prophecy is fulfilled." All of it!

Taken from my book *Twenty-Four Signs of the End Times*

The most pressing question today regarding the "Lesson of the fig tree" is, what is the timeframe where all these signs will be seen? Although Israel's spiritual eyes will not be opened until the tribulation, the visible prophetic time clock and the countdown commenced with the nation of Israel being reborn (1948). The fig tree putting out leaves is symbolic of the rebirth of Israel, partly fulfilling Ezekiel's prophecy (Ezek. 37). The nation of Israel was no longer after being desolated in 70 A.D. Not until 1948, when Israel once again became a nation, did the Jews have a homeland. Following the destruction of Jerusalem in 70 A.D., the Jews were scattered to the uttermost parts of the world. Again, in 1948 Israel was reborn in a day, fulfilling Isaiah's prophecy (Isa. 66:8). Jesus said the generation (of Jews) that sees all these signs would also see His return. In 2021, the youngest living person today that saw Israel become a nation is seventy-three years old.

When calculating the time remaining on the prophetic time clock, great care must be taken, yet sadly and often, it is not. The term 'generation' is widely misused when calculating the time remaining before Christ returns. For example, some say a generation amounts to forty years, calculated from Matthew, chapter one, which would mean Jesus would have returned in

1988. Clearly, He did not. And, if He did, the rapture would have occurred in 1981, leaving seven years of tribulation. Date setters failing with their 1981/88 interpretation reset the date to 2006/07, forty years after the six-day war (1967). Again, Jesus did not return in 2006/07; therefore, the generation that witnessed the rebirth of Israel does not apply to the forty-year theory. As mentioned above, the youngest Jews alive today, witnessing Israel's rebirth, are 73 years old, and they will still be alive to see Jesus' return. The Psalmist says, "The years of our life are seventy, or even by reason of strength eighty" (Ps. 90:10), leaving seven years left, by that calculation, for the youngest that saw the rebirth of Israel. Remember, there are seven years of tribulation following the church's rapture.

Alongside Daniel's "Seventieth week" and the "Lesson of the fig tree," Esdras' "Riddle of time" (Esd. 4:38-52) is helpful when attempting to understand the time remaining before Jesus returns, perhaps settling some frustration for those annoyed by Haggai's comment, "In a little while" (Hag. 2:6), referring to the Second Coming. The prophet Haggai said that two-thousand, five-hundred years ago, not long after Daniel was told to "Go [his] way" (Dan. 12:9, 13) because the words (prophecy) are sealed and closed until the end of time (Dan. 12:9). Even then, at the end of time, "Only the wise will understand" (Dan. 12:10).

Daniel was told to, "Go [his] way" and shut up the book until the end of time (Dan. 12:4, cf. 8:26); however, the church is told to, "Read, hear, and keep (guard) the words" (Rev. 1:3), and are further instructed, "Do not seal up the words of the prophecy of this book (Revelation), for the time is near" (Rev. 22:10). John was given the revelation (prophecy) two-thousand years ago. Due to the time between then and now, many scoffers have come, dismissing, and dismantling Bible prophecy, even from within the church (2 Pet. 3:3, Jude 1:18). Unbeknownst to them, the scoffers fulfil Bible prophecy. Anyone failing to keep the book open, failing to read, hear and keep the words of the prophecy (Rev. 1:3, 22:10), is in danger of either qualifying as a scoffer or being deceived by them. Hence, "Guard the words."

Again, the mention of, "The time being near" (Rev. 1:3) from John's revelation was two-thousand years ago, yet the lesson from the fig tree reveals, "The time is now!" As mentioned above, further confirmation is seen through Esdras' "Riddle of time" (Esd. 4:38-52). In chapter four of the book of Esdras (2), the "Apocalypse of Ezra," the angel Uriel (only seen in apocryphal texts, such as Esdras 4:1-4 and Enoch 10:1-4) was sent to Ezra to clear up some confusion and frustration regarding the ways of God (Esd. 4:2, 11). The angel was sent to help him understand, like Daniel (Dan. 8:16-17, 9:22-23, 25, 10:10-14).

The angel Uriel asked Ezra three questions (Esd. 4:5):

1. Can you weigh fire?
2. Can you measure the wind?
3. Can you recall the days past?

Ezra answers by saying, "No man can" (Esd. 4:6). Uriel continues by rising (not asking) five more questions (Esd. 4:7):

4. How many chambers are in the midst of the sea?
5. How many springs are in the beginnings of the deep?
6. How much water is above the firmament?
7. What are the outlets of Sheol?
8. What are the paths of Paradise?

The angel asks the questions to point out that Ezra is ignorant of God, His ways, and His creation. The rebuke is like Job's, chapter thirty-eight

(Job. 38:4-41), where God put Job in his place by asking, "What do you know, and what can you do?" Paul said something similar in Romans chapter nine (Rom. 9:20). The answers to God's questions of Job are, "What do you know?" and "What can you do?" is next to nothing. The same is true of Uriel's questioning of Ezra and Paul's of the church of Rome. The point is, do not question God! The corrupted cannot completely understand the incorruptible (Esd. 4:11).

Although Ezra knew about the first three questions, he could not answer them. Ezra had no knowledge of the following five questions, therefore had no chance of answering any questions about them. Neither could he understand why God made some to live in sin and suffer eternally, which was what troubled Ezra (Esd. 4:12, cf. chapter 3), which again, is like Paul's rebuke in the book of Romans (Rom. 9:20), also taking about a remnant that will be saved (Rom. 9:27).

In the following verses (Esd. 4:13-18), Uriel presents Ezra with a foolish situation, to which Ezra rightly judges it to be ridiculous (Esd. 4:19). This was confirmed by the angel (Esd. 4:20a), who further makes the point, "Why then do you not judge yourself in the same way," wisely? (Esd. 4:20b). Only God, who is above the earth, and incorruptible, can understand the matters Ezra was frustrated with (Esd. 4:21). Recognising the foolishness of his ways (Esd. 4:23), knowing, "We are not worthy of mercy" (Esd. 4:24), Ezra asked for understanding (Esd. 4:22).

Uriel answers, "The more you search, the more you will marvel because the world is quickly passing away" (Esd. 4:26). The things to come cannot come until this world has run its course, and the promises of God cannot coexist with the current corruption of humanity (Esd. 4:27-29). The question then remains, "How long?" (Esd. 4:33). Before Uriel gives the "Riddle of time" (Esd. 4:38-52), he cautions Ezra, "Do not try to hurry the Most

High" (Esd. 4:34), again referring to what is outside of Ezra's understanding, asking:

1. Did not the souls of the righteous ask about these things in their chambers, saying, "How long will we be here?"
2. "When does the harvest of our reward come?"

Uriel informed Ezra that he answered the souls in Paradise, "Until the number is complete" (cf. Rev. 6:11).

The time has already been decided by the times and the number of seasons, which cannot be changed until the full number comes in (Esd. 4:27). When the time comes, it will be like a pregnant woman giving birth, even if she wanted to, she could not withhold (Esd. 4:40, cf. 1 Thess. 5:3).

After explaining that nothing can stop what will happen in the future, the mystery of the amount of time left is given to Ezra. By looking back to creation (Esd. 4:43) and calculating the time since Ezra is told the time remaining is less (Esd. 4:43-50), nothing more can be said about it (Esd. 4:52). Ezra, like Daniel, was too far outside of the last day's timeframe to understand; however, we are not, and can solve the riddle.

The riddle of time outlines prophecy from creation to the Messianic kingdom, with verses forty-four to fifty (Esd. 4:44-50) providing a prophetic timeline. There has been more time from the world's creation to Ezra's existence than from Ezra to the Messianic kingdom (Esd. 4:45, 50), established on the return of Jesus Christ. Ezra lived between 480-440 BC. Ken Johnson (Th.D.), a Bible prophecy lecturer and Christian author, states that from the time of Ezra, there were 3925, and the time before Ezra was around three thousand, four hundred years (3,445-3485 years). If that amount of time is more than what remains, then the return of Jesus Christ must occur before 3005-3045 AD. Then, by subtracting one thousand years of the Messianic kingdom, somewhere between 2005-2045 A.D. would be the timeframe remaining.

Johnson concluded by calculating that the first part of the riddle is from creation to 480 BC., and the second is from 480 BC. to an AD—date. The missing four hundred plus years is on the AD—date from its starting point, four hundred, plus years BC.

My approach to the calculation is slightly different from Johnson's, starting from the time of Ezra, from creation (3485), less the years of Ezra (midpoint) until Christ (460), less the years from Christ to current day (2023), (=5968, with 32 years remaining before the start of the millennium, the seventh day). By adding thirty-two years to the year 2023, the year of Christ's return could be 2055 A.D. Then subtract seven years for the tribulation, placing the rapture in the year 2048. Precisely one hundred years after the rebirth of Israel (1948). The calculation works with less time from Ezra to the resurrection (2055) (Esd. 45, 50) than from the time that has already passed (3485).

A similar timeframe is given by Enoch, in his book (Enoch), chapters ninety-one to ninety-three (Enoch 91-93), known as the 'Apocalypse of Weeks', Enoch states the prophecies will be fulfilled between 1975 and 2075 A.D.

Enoch was the seventh generation of Adam and lived for three hundred and sixty-five years before being raptured into heaven (Gen. 5:1-24, Heb. 11:5-6). Enoch gave birth to Methuselah (Gen. 5), who died the same week before the Flood (Gen. 7:1-4). While the book of Enoch is considered to be part of the apocryphal books, it is given credibility through the book of Jude, stating that "He prophesied, saying, "Behold, the Lord comes with ten thousand of his holy ones" (Jude 1:14, Enoch 1:9). Like with Esdras, early church fathers considered the book of Enoch to be authentic, such as Irenaeus, Origen, Tertullian, Anatolius, Theodotus, and Flavius Josephus.

Legend has it that Enoch gave his book to Noah, who took it onto the ark, then passed it down the line through Shem and the tribe of Levi. To preserve it, the Essenes buried it., along with other ancient texts, later found, in full, among the Dead Sea Scrolls in 1956 written in Aramaic. The book of Enoch (1) was also preserved by the Ethiopian Christian Church and remained part of the Ethiopian Bible. In 1893 the book was translated from the Ethiopic language to English.

Because the books of Esdras and Enoch are apocryphal books, the prophesies need to be tested and filtered through the modern Bible despite the opening argument supporting their credibility. The lesson from the fig tree is the prominent place and tool to test Ezra's calendarized prediction.

As mentioned earlier, Israel is symbolic of the fig tree, rebirthed in 1948. Jesus said that the generation that witnesses Israel's rebirth will see His return, the youngest now seventy-three/four years old. At the turn of the century, the youngest was fifty-two years old; therefore, the endpoint of Enoch's prophecy (2075) is too far out. A generation is not one hundred and twenty-seven years. However, Johnson's calculation of Ezra's prediction fits with his prophetic endpoint of 2045, making the youngest living Jew ninety-seven years old when Jesus returns. Yet, seven years of tribulation still need to be subtracted for the church, predicting the rapture to occur, at the latest, around 2038 A.D. At the latest, according to Johnson, the church will be removed from the earth within fifteen years from now. By my calculation, according to the prophecy, Jesus could return for His church somewhere around, or before, the year 1948, precisely one hundred years after the rebirth of Israel. *Remember, no one knows the day or the hour (Matt. 24:42, 44, 50, 25:13). We are not date setting but rather, speculating.

In conclusion, the prophet Zechariah saw some two thousand five hundred years into the future when revealing the things to come - the tribulation, the Messiah's arrival (the Second Coming), and the Messianic kingdom. While the revelation for him was many days from his lifetime, like Daniel's, the prophecies will be fulfilled within ours, "In a little while" (Hag. 2:9). Indeed, "The time is near" (Rev. 1:3), much nearer than most realise, and will take the majority by surprise, as predicted (Lu. 17:26-37, 21:34, 1 Thess. 5:3). Swiftly following the shock and horror of the masses, who scoffed at prophecy, will be their judgment (2 Thess. 1:9).

ABOUT THE AUTHOR

Marc R. Wheway, Ph.D., is the founder and director of Kingdom Seekers., and the pastor of Kingdom Seekers Wesleyan Methodist Church on the Gold Coast, Australia. Kingdom Seekers is an eschatological ministry focused on preparing the bride of Christ for the return of Christ. Dr. Wheway has earned a Ph.D., majoring in eschatology, through Louisiana Baptist University and Theological Seminary, complemented by a Master's degree in International Relations through Griffith University. Dr. Wheway also has an MBA through the Australian Institute of Business, which is further complemented with a Master's degree in Employment (Industrial) Relations through Griffith University.

www.ingramcontent.com/pod-product-compliance
Lightning Source LLC
Chambersburg PA
CBHW060533100426
42743CB00009B/1516